Enjoy!

Tony

Do You Know Me?

By

Tony Roberts

for my daughter

Table of Contents

Why an Actor?

"Tony Roberts. Still around!"

The woman, around fifty, in a shabby coat stepped out of a doorway on Broadway and 44th Street as I was wending my way uptown after giving a performance in a play. I don't remember what play it was, but it had been running for a while, and I do remember that she proclaimed it loudly enough to be heard at least a block away:

"Tony Roberts. Still around!"

I was in my early forties at the time and didn't quite know how to respond. She didn't need a response, because she was already gone, but I did feel a need to evaluate this unsought assessment and file it in its proper place. Shouldn't I have been flattered by the fact that she recognized me at all?

I've never been particularly lucky at card games, I've never hit a jackpot, but I have been extremely lucky in life. Unlike many of my pals who didn't know what they wanted to become when they "grew up," I knew I wanted to be an actor before I got to high school. My friends and I enacted all the best scenes from the films we loved, having memorized our favorite dialogue. My happiest hours were spent dueling with imaginary swords up and down the alleys of Yorkville a la the Gene Kelly version of The Three Musketeers. We pointed cap guns at each other and staged shoot-outs on fire escapes. I would hurl myself with tremendous velocity against a brick wall as if struck by a volley of bullets from James Cagney's machine gun. I died hanging over the rim of a garbage can. It was best to do this at a bus stop because then there were people standing there to see it.

Being a teenager in the 1950's meant that you lived to go to the movies. There were new films to see every weekend, forty cents to get in the door, and they ranged from war pictures to Biblical epics and MGM musicals. The world in the movies became as real as the mundane repetition of everyday life. There was also a program on television called The Million Dollar Movie, which would replay the same film twice each evening for an entire week. That way, I could really learn the lines and repeat them when circumstances made it amusing to do so, at least to me.

I would pretend to get shot at the top of the giant stairway at the RKO 86th Street Theatre and grope my way falteringly to the lobby, where I was usually met by the head usher and led to the nearest exit. But while being thrown out, it occurred to me that certain "grownups" were getting paid for what they were pretending, and were admired for doing so by millions of satisfied customers. It seemed like an ideal way to make a living.

I was born on October 22, 1939, at Lenox Hill Hospital located on Manhattan's Upper East Side, the first child of loving and happily married parents. We weren't rich, but "upper middle class" as my father would describe us. My father, Ken Roberts, was a successful radio announcer whose voice was familiar to millions of listeners across the country. Radio was in its heyday from 1932 to 1950, after which television would become the medium of choice. My dad was the host of such hit programs as Quick As A Flash, Let's Pretend, It Pays To Be Ignorant, The Shadow, You Are There, and many others. Whenever I got to stay home from school because of a cold or sore throat, I listened to them on the radio.

My father believed acting to be a heroic endeavor but an impractical pursuit. He would have preferred me to choose a more secure future by becoming a doctor or lawyer. He had left law school himself at age twenty to become an actor, and he made it to Broadway in an early flop written by Garson Kanin, who wrote Born Yesterday several years later. The play closed quickly, and after winning an audition to become a staff announcer at CBS, he never went back to work in the theatre. He loved actors and spent decades of his life in the service of The American Federation of Radio and Television Artists (AFTRA), where he helped create The Screen Actor's Guild. Sources vary as to his first job; it was either in New Jersey in the late 1920s, or at Brooklyn's WLTH in 1930, but what is clear is that he had a long, distinguished career. His obituary in The New York Times went on: "Roberts was one of the leading lights of radio. He had no regional accent, but was still distinctive, authoritative, and reassuring. His voice might not have sounded ethnic, but his roots were. Roberts was the son of Jewish immigrants. His mother, the former Fanny Naft, came from what is now the Ukraine. His father, Nathaniel Trochman, an insurance salesman and an English tutor for other Eastern European immigrants, hailed from Latvia."

Before he became an announcer, my father worked briefly as an unpaid intern in the law office of the future Mayor of New York City, Fiorello LaGuardia. One day, he asked to be compensated for his car fare to and from work in order to spare his parents, who were poor, the added expense of his transportation. He was turned down, so he quit. Interesting to note is that the name "Roberts," which replaced "Trochman" has its origins in North Wales, deriving from the Anglo-Saxon/Norman name "Roberts" meaning "bright fame." My father had never even been to Wales.

My father, born Saul Trochman, was a man who first and foremost believed in the golden rule: "Do unto others as you would have others do unto you." He taught that concept with great fervor. Proud of his Jewish heritage, he considered us to be reformed Jews. We didn't belong to a temple or attend services, but nevertheless I saw him as the most moral and upright man I ever knew (although on a few occasions, as I was leaving our apartment to go to school, I bumped into him at the front door coming home from an all-night poker game). According to my mother, or at least what he told her, he never won or lost but conveniently broke even. That way he could pocket his winnings, if he had any, while never endangering the family budget if he lost. Other than that, his behavior was so beyond reproach that I wonder, in retrospect, if he was compensating for a ghost in the family closet, as it were. I chalked it up to the usual guilt that comes with the territory when you're Jewish (perhaps Survivor's Guilt.) It wouldn't be until well into my own middle age that I would learn about the something in the family archives to cause this shame.

Jump to 2011. I'm leaning on the rail of a cruise ship as it maneuvers through the narrow strait flowing into the port of Riga, the capital of Latvia, on the Baltic Sea. As we passed the lighthouse on the way in, it occurred to me that this must have been the last thing my paternal grandfather saw when he left to immigrate to America in 1887. He was seventeen at the time and only passed that lighthouse once. He never went back, and neither did my father, born in New York City twenty-three years later. The story has it that with only twenty dollars in his pocket he managed to reach Copenhagen, and soon after arrived at Ellis Island. There may, or may not, have been a relative there to meet him. Nobody knows. His name was Nachman Trochman, altered by the customs officers who changed his first name to Nathaniel. I know all this because my younger sister, Nancy Roberts, was more curious about our past than I was. She made the effort to find the ship's boarding records in the annals of

New York's historical archives and gave a printout of the original to my father on the occasion of his eighty-fifth birthday. We were both surprised by his indifference to it which has led me to surmise that in keeping with other aspects of his relationship to the far past, he would rather forget the whole thing.

There has always been a suspicion expressed by some of my now-departed relatives that at some point in my grandfather's life (perhaps when he was collecting loans for Macy's Department Store) either he or his partner at the time were caught in a scheme that led to his spending a year in prison for embezzling money from his employers. My grandfather went missing for a year but, according to my father, it was due to his being so desperate for money that he had gone to work for a distant cousin in St. Louis until he was able to amass enough funds to return to the family. In the meantime, my father and grandmother were evicted from their meager apartment on the Lower East Side of Manhattan and had to find work. They were used to moving frequently because of a practice that permitted families to live rent-free for a full month before the rent came due. (Many families at the time relocated every four weeks.) I still don't know if this story was invented by my father to shield me from the truth or whether it was what he actually believed. What I do know is that my father preached the principles of good citizenship and made every attempt to live an honorable life. He may have succeeded too well for my own good, as I often felt that I would never be able to live up to his high standards. He was a bit like the father in John Steinbeck's East of Eden, seeking perfection in himself and those most dear to him. He protected me from knowing about the specific hardships of his generation. We held Seders on Passover, but they didn't dwell on the relentless tragedy of our people. They were gatherings filled with laughter and good cheer. My sister and I never heard the word "Holocaust" until we were teenagers.

All these thoughts ran through my mind as I watched the lighthouse come into view. What must it have been like to be Nachman Trochman? How daring it must have been to leave his family and travel to a land where the people spoke a different language. He probably did it in order to avoid being drafted into the Russian Army. Nobody knows. Despite the mistakes he may or may not have made in his earlier years, he would achieve respectability by becoming the President of the Greater New York Aid Society. He died when I was only seven years-old, so my recollection of him is hazy, at best, and the images I have of him are mostly from crinkled black and white photographs. I am an infant in Fanny's arms and he is smiling down at me. He was married to the same woman all his life, who arrived in America when she was six from Odessa, a port in the south of Russia. They met each other in a belt factory in the Bronx where they worked and had an only son, Saul Trochman, my father.

Fanny Naft was the most "gemütlich" presence in my childhood.

gemütlich;
cozy, agreeable, and cheerful

She occasionally spoke some Yiddish, played cards with me when she babysat, and spent a lot of her time making blintzes, or working for Hadassah. I can't think about Fanny without welling up inside. She took me to see Charlie Chaplin movies after school in the basement of The Museum of Modern Art. She also took me to the Statue of Liberty. I was eight or nine and she was in her sixties, but we both made it all the way up to the crown.

One evening, Fanny walked from the West Side to the East Side by using the transverse, or highway, that allows traffic to go back and forth through Central Park. There is a narrow unlit curb along the side of this thoroughfare, but its only purpose is in case of an emergency. After my grandfather died, Fanny had often taken this route as a way of avoiding the cost of a bus or taxi, which were the only alternatives. My father found out, and it was the first and only time I ever saw him lose his temper. He was angry because we were well-off enough that she didn't need to take such a risk. It was already dark and nobody ever went into the park at night. His voice jumped an octave as he pleaded with her not to do it again. She lived in a small apartment two floors below her widowed sister on Columbus Avenue and 75th Street. She was one of three sisters who often quarreled for one reason or another, but her invitations to them were always the same: "You can come or not come, but if you come, come pleasant!" When Fanny died, she left a bank account with around $9,000 in it; money she had saved out of her monthly allowance from my father.

Because of Fanny's persistence, I felt obligated to attend Sunday School. It didn't matter much to my parents either way, but my father thought it would be good for me to be exposed to the story of "our people." He left the choice up to me. I went to Sunday School for one year and was confirmed at Temple Emanuel located just off Central Park at 65th Street. I wasn't crazy about it. The kids who went there came and went by limousine, while I locked up my bike in the vestibule. Some of my closest friends had been going to Sunday School since the third grade and I attended their Bar Mitzvahs, but could hardly wait until they were over. I felt I owed it to my grandmother to graduate from Sunday School, even if I never had a Bar Mitzvah. I know she forgives me for that, just as she forgave me for cheating at Gin Rummy and Casino.

My mother's family, the Finklesteins, were relatively well-to-do, at least until the stock market crashed in 1929, after which they were forced to adjust to a more frugal lifestyle. They also wanted to assimilate to America, but maintained a distrust that they would ever feel truly safe here. My maternal grandmother, whose father was a Rabbi, told me she was smuggled out of the Ukraine under a pile of hay in a donkey cart. Their history led them to believe that it wasn't smart to trust any place, no matter how much money one could make in the garment industry. Grandma Anne tried to preserve her heritage without calling too much attention to it. At seventeen, she was coerced (for financial reasons) to marry into a family with a dominating father and five sons. She was, quite literally, the poor relative, and she came to resent it bitterly after they lost most of their money in the crash.

My mother's older brother, Bob Finklestein, navigated airplanes over the Pacific while fighting the Japanese during World War II. He was always in a uniform in the photographs I saw of him. A decorated war hero, and highly esteemed by the whole family for his service to the country.

After the war he attended Georgia Tech, became an engineer, and went to work for RCA, the Radio Corporation of America. At some point, the Air Force was having some problems with the Atlas Missile: there was no way to tell exactly how much fuel remained in the missile after it had been launched. A model of the Atlas was sent to him by The Pentagon so that he could study it before full production went forward. He showed it to me in his backyard. He solved the problem by using sound waves to measure the exact amount of fuel remaining in the missile at any given time. A few years later he invented a way to use ultrasonic sound waves to finely clean everything from surgical instruments to expensive jewelry, and anything in-between. When he was in his nineties, he formulated a way to kill bugs and other garden pests (perhaps some Japanese beetles) in an environmentally-friendly way.

Growing up, he also kept a vast number of complicated engineering structures in his room. My mother, his sister, often explained that his extraordinary intelligence and curiosity in all things technological created an intimidating array of radio speakers and receivers that kept his room off limits to the usual tending and primping of most homes. In other words, his mother and sister were afraid to go into his room.

My mother was the most sophisticated woman I have ever known. She attended the Calhoun School and later Hunter College, although she quit after two years to study shorthand and other secretarial skills. She became a "girl Friday" for Max Fleischer, who founded Biograph Studios in Queens and produced the *Popeye* and *Betty Boop* cartoons. But she still had a hand in show business. One of her tasks was to hold the long black pole that bounced on top of the lyrics in the "follow the bouncing ball" shorts that were popular at the time. She had a great sense of humor, and believed that laughter could get anybody through anything. She loved to cook, knew what good Jazz was, and ardently read Dickens, Proust, and Mark Twain.

After one of my early stage appearances, she told me I had this unique quality as a performer that drew the audiences attention.

"I don't know why, but I can't look at anyone else on the stage."

"Mom," I explained, "you're only looking at me because you're my mother! Every other mother in the theatre is only watching their son or daughter."

"Not true. It's something special. It's an energy that you project. When you smile, it lights up the whole theatre."

I took it with a grain of salt. She also loved to tell family and friends that I sat, transfixed, when the soundtrack from Laurence Olivier's film *Henry V* was broadcast over the airwaves. The orchestral arrangements suggested streams of arrows whistling through the sky while Olivier's crisp and perfect diction worked its magic on my eight year-old imagination. To this day, I'm not sure if I actually remember listening to it, or only imagine it because of my mother's retelling. I *do* know that I can still recite every word of the "St. Crispin" speech that spurred Henry's army into battle. He was a leader of men, a winner against all odds. I was inspired to become either Olivier, or Henry V. It didn't matter which.

In the photos taken of my mother before my birth, she resembles a well-coiffed movie star, like Loretta Young, but she had never aspired to be an actress. In her later years, she was invited to contribute her estimable wit to the writer's group that wrote *The Tonight Show*, but she declined. She didn't have a particularly competitive spirit and in her middle age, didn't wish to develop one. According to her, W.C. Fields and Groucho Marx were the funniest men who ever lived, French and Italian food were the best, and she was never happy unless she finished the Times crossword puzzle in ink. I rarely saw her at breakfast because it was too early in the day for her to be awake. I was given bacon and cream cheese sandwiches by our housekeeper, after she cleared away the empty glasses from the social goings-on of the night before. I was asked by the principle of my grade school to have my mother come to school with me the next morning because of my frequent lateness. I said that was impossible because my mother seldom got out of bed until noon. I believe they worked things out over the phone. (She once wrote a letter of complaint to Frank E. Schattuck, the President of Schrafft's, because she had been served an ice cream soda without a spoon!)

"Take your complaints right to the top," she advised. "If Bloomingdales doesn't deliver the goods on time, then it is best to call the president of the store. Never hassle with underlings. If the right people hear about your displeasure, there's a better chance you'll get results."

She was full of aphorisms:

"Never wear anything with a label on it."

"A room never looks as small as when there is nothing in it."

"Only the nouveau riche travel with expensive luggage."

"For good or bad, the sexiest sound in the world is the creak of a floorboard in an adulterer's bedroom."

"Everybody has faults. If you expect your friends not to have faults, you are destined to end up without any friends."

She would keep some small trifle in a drawer, or closet, in order to present it as a gift to some unexpected visitor at holiday time. She would gift wrap it so that they would have something to open. She may not have been much of a hugger, but she loved Dickens because of his sympathy for the poor, and Lewis Carroll for his sense of the absurd.

She also believed that the next World War would be the end of everything and that it would ultimately be blamed on the Jews. During World War II, she volunteered to read letters to injured servicemen at local Veteran's Hospitals and acted as a Nurse's Aide.

My father was far more involved and intimate with me. He sat on the edge of my bed and assured me that my gifts and talents, as he called them, were every bit as worthy and admirable as the abilities I lacked. I was in need of consolation because I was clumsy in the outfield and slow on the bases. I was in need of pep talks after failing miserably, in my mind, to compete with my peers or achieve any kind of respect as an athlete. I spent a sleepless night in my bunk at camp on parents' weekend after being assigned to play in the baseball competition. I was positioned in right field because nothing ever happened there. It was the least active spot on the roster and I bungled the only opportunity I had to catch a ball. I also struck out three times. I felt deeply ashamed, but my father was always there to encourage me. It was he who checked to see that I wore my rubbers in the rain. Eventually, my mother, my sister, and I labeled him the Original Jewish Mother.

Nancy, born six years after me, brought a new dynamic into the mix, to say the least. In the family mythology, I was born easy and was of good humor. My mother suffered from a miscarriage and a stillborn child before my sister arrived, but Nancy was difficult to manage from the start. Despite her superior intellect, (superior to mine, anyway) she had emotional issues that surfaced, both at home and at school. In Fourth Grade, it was recommended that she transfer to a school with specialized educators who knew how to support and teach social education as well as academic education. Her life was a constant battle against weight-gain, which may have contributed to her death from cancer at the age of sixty-four. In spite of her ordeals, she went on to become a well known television host in England for several years and wrote a much heralded book titled, *Breaking All the Rules.* It became required reading at many colleges and was far ahead of its time, as it deals with the demoralizing affects that the diet and fashion industries have on women.

I was the golden boy. I had it all. But I had my own weight issues. I was taken to a specialist when I was twelve and prescribed thyroid pills, which eventually allowed me to lose almost thirty pounds in two months, but it didn't matter. My self-image was set. I was convinced I was too fat to compete against my peers.

The closest I ever came to experiencing the war in Europe and the

Pacific was in Central Park during a U.S. Army battle demonstration, calculated to sell war bonds. The sound of the explosions was deafening and there were soldiers crawling under barbed wire and shooting tracer bullets at an enormous tank. Coupled with the air raid sirens that I heard at night during practice blackouts throughout the city, it was difficult to realize that the war was overseas. Passing traffic in the darkened streets would cast shadows through the venetian blinds onto the ceiling of my bedroom, and it scared me. I was lucky I couldn't read the newspapers, but I still heard the sounds of warfare in the background of radio news reports. That said, what I could grasp was positive. We were winning the war and things would turn out all right.

Not far from this make-believe combat zone there is a wooden bench I still enjoy visiting. There exists a short film of me sitting happily on that same bench, only I'm on my mother's lap. My father shot this two-minute epic with his new 16mm motion picture camera in order to record the moment for the family's future posterity. My grandparents were there, too, in all their Sunday finery.

My father could become quite antic when he was directing home movies with his 16mm camera. He would assume the role of Oscar Jaffe, played by John Barrymore in *Twentieth Century*. He actually resembled Barrymore, worshiped him, and brought a dramatic grandeur to his demeanor with faces and gestures to equal those of "the great profile" himself. I thought I was the luckiest kid in the world to have him as a father. We'd go swimming in the ocean off of Ocean Beach on Fire Island, and I would boast to the other kids about how my dad was on the radio. As far as I was concerned, he was the spitting image of Errol Flynn, who played Robin Hood in the movies. How much better could it get? Robin Hood was my dad! He lived to be ninety-nine and, except for a few knee replacements, was in relatively good health. This is surprising because he ate whatever he liked and didn't believe in strenuous exercise (although, he did ride his bike to the studio every day when he was the announcer for the soap operas, *The Secret*

Storm and *Love of Life*.) In those days, when soaps were aired live, he had a lot of extra time on his hands and spent it productively. He taught himself Italian, read the Times thoroughly, and studied gardening well enough to produce an award-winning rose in his tiny garden in Ocean Beach. He had a tireless energy and was curious about everything throughout his life.

My father was a tough act to follow. He'd had all of the struggles, while I seemed to be dealt all the cards. I wanted to succeed and I wanted him to be proud of me. I would have to be something big to be *me*.

On the bus to boot camp years later, at the start of the Vietnam War, I gazed out the window at the dreary landscape and decided I needed to be someone else. "Who would that be?" I wondered. I chose to be Gregory Peck because of the strong, silent resolve of the characters he played, especially when under stress. He could be momentarily humiliated by the bad guys, but in the final accounting, he always reclaimed his heroic stature and came out a winner. *That's* who I wanted to be! The strategy worked too well. After eight weeks of basic training, my company chose me by a secret ballot as the trooper they would most readily follow into battle. I was stunned, but presumed that this honor fell on me because I would be the last person they would expect to go, unless there was absolutely no alternative. Fortunately, the occasion never presented itself. Nevertheless, I was assigned to train new recruits how to shoot a flamethrower and how to fire at low-flying aircraft using a 50-caliber machine gun. I had never done that before, nor wanted to, but I had seen Burt Lancaster do it in *From Here to Eternity*. So I just pretended to be him.

As I got older, I was taken to the studios, or in some cases the theatres, where my dad's programs were performed and broadcast. These outings had a tremendous influence on me. I was transfixed and enchanted. I met professional actors dressed like ordinary businessmen and women, wearing jackets and ties, who transformed themselves into imaginary characters. They poured their voices into little metal contraptions called microphones, while their faces and bodies reflected the dramatic tensions of the story line. These grownups really believed in what they were saying and having a lot of fun doing it. They were creating a world that didn't exist. How could I not want to be one of them? They may have never known where their next paycheck was coming from, but when they went to work, they went to pretend. I could begin to imagine that with the right clothes and props I, too, could convince an audience that I was anybody I chose to be.

The actors were my heroes because they spent their days pretending to be people other than themselves. They wanted desperately to persuade the listeners to believe in the stories they were telling. They also did everything within reason to discourage me from following in their footsteps.

"You don't want to be lookin' for a job all the time, do you kid?"

"Why don't you do something worthwhile and have a good life?"

"It's no fun to be lookin' for a job when you're middle-aged."

But they were pursuing a lost cause. They missed the point. I wanted to be exactly like them!

My parents loved the theatre and started taking me to shows when I was about six. The first was Orson Welles' *Around the World in Eighty Days*. The production was a great spectacle. The curtain fell, and the actors took their bows. Welles, still in-character as Phileas Fogg, stepped downstage, aimed a double barreled shotgun at the chandelier hanging over the audience, and pulled the trigger. My seat shook and my ears rang as wisps of smoke hung in the air. Immediately, hundreds of multicolored feathers fell from above. I was hooked.

While still in elementary school, I enrolled in an acting class at the 92nd Street Young Men's Hebrew Association (YMHA). We didn't speak Hebrew in our family, and neither did most of the kids who went there for extracurricular activities. We were cast in a staged reenactment of *George Washington Crossing the Delaware*. We studied the famous painting closely, and molded ourselves into their silhouettes. We morphed into a group of soldiers huddled together in a small boat (a few arranged chairs), and with the teacher's prodding tried to imagine what they must have felt like. It would have been dark, and cold, and they were probably scared to death, but these early Americans were determined to make it to the far shore, and they did. And I got to play George Washington! This didn't stop my mother from calling the YMHA to complain that I had not been given a speaking role, since I had begun acting classes several weeks previously. Jessica Walter, who later achieved stardom in many films, was in my class. She commuted from Queens.

By the age of seven or eight, I presumed myself to be the most sensitive kid in the room. I was sensitive to my own feelings and to the feelings of anyone else I perceived to be disadvantaged, including the kids who got bullied on the way to school, were picked on by intimidating teachers, or were robbed of their candy at Halloween. It occurred to me every so often that I might just be the second coming of Christ.

On Halloween I would collect goodies from the neighbors and nearby buildings.

Once in the streets, I became vulnerable to gangs. These were groups of teenagers, mostly from recent immigrant families, who roamed the outskirts of affluent neighborhoods. They were unlike today's organized gangs, commonly associated with drugs and criminal activity. On one occasion I was chased by a group of bad guys, and sought mercy from a woman in a passing taxi. She opened the passenger door and let me in as the cab paused at a stoplight on Madison Avenue. I got in, thanked her, and got out at the next corner. From there, it was only a few yards to the entrance of my building. I had escaped a scary situation, even though we lived in a relatively good neighborhood.

After three years at the progressive School of Ethical Culture, a private school on Manhattan's West Side which had failed to teach me to read, I was transferred to Public School 6 on the East Side. Between those enrollments, I spent a year at The Rogers School in Stamford, Connecticut. My family decided to try the suburbs. It was the thing to do at the time. My mother hated to drive and felt housebound compared to the flexibility of the life she'd led in the city. As for me, I was "the new boy" in class among classmates who had a history with each other, and was trying to adjust to an environment completely unfamiliar to me. We lived in a large colonial-style house on an acre of land, with its own beach and a two-car garage.

Some time around the fifth grade I started taking piano lessons. I loved the piano and music of all kinds. I liked the orchestral dissonance of the great Russian composers like Stravinsky, Prokovief, and Shostokovitch, yet our forebears had fled Russia as if from the plague. Go figure. I didn't have the same passion for the piano as I did for acting. I would skip the assigned scale exercises, which I found tedious, but plod slowly through passages of *Rhapsody in Blue* which were far too difficult. It didn't matter. I got such joy from playing the right chord every once in a while that I still got pleasure out of it. I play today, but only when no one is around, and I feel sorry for the neighbors. I did play the Marvin Hamlisch character in *They're Playing Our Song* on Broadway for almost a year, and opened each performance seated behind a grand piano accompanying myself as I sang the opening number. I was singing, of course, but inside the piano there was only air and plywood. The pianist in the orchestra tickled the ivories in the pit while my hands moved back and forth over silent keys.

One morning, my mother told me that she and my father had visited some friends nearby. After dinner, a boy, about fourteen years-old, came downstairs in his pajamas, said goodnight to the guests and, before going upstairs to bed, played *Rhapsody in Blue* from memory without a single mistake. His name was Stephen Sondheim. Fifty years later I was cast in an all-star production of *Follies* at The Papermill Playhouse in New Jersey. Sondheim said he remembered both the evening and my parents. If I had been there, I might never have touched the piano again.

By thinking I might be Christ (I think I mentioned that was an early fantasy I never shared, Thank God), and later wanting to lead the poorly armed and outnumbered English troops, as Henry V had done against the French at Agincourt, I set heroic aspirations for myself. In the real world I was the first to talk my way out of a fight. It just seemed like the practical thing to do. Why get hurt? I was happy to move back to the city when my father sold the house in Stamford. I felt surer of myself in the city, despite the dangers of Central Park.

You could say that I grew up in Central Park, which is saying a lot, because the park is a vast stretch of space in Manhattan and has become the tourist center of the city in recent years. It was not always so. It was once quaint, but forbidding. It was the forest that Grandpa warned Peter not to venture into in *Peter and the Wolf.* In the park I discovered the famous pond where my first hero, Stuart Little, won his challenging sailboat race. I borrowed that book out of the school library during the third grade and used the last two empty pages to write a happier ending than the one E.B. White provided. I wanted Stuart to find Margalo, a sparrow he had befriended, when he set out to find her in his tiny car, dwarfed by the enormous forest as shown in the sketch on the last page. It wasn't optimistic enough for me. I wasn't tiny like Stuart Little, but for some reason I identified with him and was inspired by his ambitious spirit. As a consequence of adding my addendum in ink, my library card was suspended.

The park was the place to pass time, play ball, ride a bike, and roam through open space. There was a reservoir, a bridle path with real horses, basketball and tennis courts, and hot dog vendors. At first, I only went there with my parents, or was taken by my nurse to play on the lawn or sit on a seesaw. My crowning folly was to ignore the advice, offered by a passing policeman, that I not lean too far over the edge of the sailboat pond as I tried to fill a Crackerjack box with water. The bottom of the cement pond loomed up at me as I plummeted straight down. He heard the splash and was near enough to grab me by the seat of my pants and yank me back to solid ground. As if that wasn't embarrassing enough, I was forced to get out of my wet clothes and put on a dress some other kid's nanny had brought along as a spare. I was seven. This wouldn't be the last time in my life that I would be asked to wear a dress. There would be three more times, all on Broadway, but more of that later. Oh, alright, the second dress was worn in *Sugar* and the third in *Victor/Victoria.*

Harlem was off limits and seemed like a million miles away. Anyone familiar with the city in the years of my youth knew that 96th Street was a border. There were political and demographic reasons for this, but the truth was that none of us knew what might happen to us north of that perimeter. If the pink rubber High Bounce ball we used for street games accidentally found its way to the other side of the street, one of us would go upstairs and bring down a replacement.

Perhaps those fears of confrontation help explain why the culture of gangster films and "shoot-'em-ups" made such a vivid impression on my pals and me. They gave us a chance to pretend that we were tougher and braver than we actually were. We could do imitations of anybody who acted tough, but we were never confrontational with anybody ourselves, except for my friend Marty Coppersmith. He challenged a guy who bumped his shoulder as they passed each other on Park Avenue—Marty acted tough, but he took a left hook to the jaw he never expected. He was too stunned to respond and we led him away from a humiliating encounter. I decided it was much better to *act* tough and not get hurt doing it.

Meanwhile, my father continued to urge me to consider going into a more stable profession.

"Why take the chance? Think of how comfortable you could be if you were a doctor!"

But I preferred to have the chance to pretend to be a doctor. I wanted to play cowboys, gangsters, athletes, detectives, presidents, and legends of American culture, like Tom Sawyer and Abraham Lincoln. Needless to say, these types were not usually of ethnic origin. Even years later, Neil Simon would ask me to straighten my hair when I replaced Robert Redford in *Barefoot in the Park* on Broadway. I was cast as Paul Bratter, husband of Cory, who, to use the vernacular of the time, looked like "white bread city." My hair was straightened for eighteen months, after which I was lucky to have any hair left at all.

My father's idealism and belief in America was expressed, in part, by his enthusiasm for baseball. He was a devout fan. He loved the New York Giants and spent much of his youth standing on Coogan's Bluff just beyond the Polo Grounds. After Jackie Robinson joined the Brooklyn Dodgers, baseball was a game where talent and skill prevailed regardless of anyone's creed, or color. It was truly a level playing field. As I grew up, we went to games together like so many other fathers and sons. We went to Giants games and shared the Bobby Thompson home run miracle that won the pennant in 1951. We had the car radio tuned to the game as we drove uptown on Central Park West. As Thompson came to the plate, my father was too excited to maneuver through the traffic and pulled over to the curb where we parked with the engine running until our jubilation broke out. Perhaps that explains why my most constant soporific for the first third of my life was me hitting a baseball so hard that it would travel the length of any diamond ever imagined and produce a home run. *That* would be the ultimate achievement.

But the ride from the Polo Grounds brought a rude awakening. We drove through the local streets of Harlem on the way to our apartment past a world utterly foreign to me. The houses were in a state of decline and disrepair that I couldn't understand, or that couldn't be excused. I was a public school student after the third grade and had Black and Latino friends, but I had never seen an entire race congregated in such an ominous and unnatural setting. It didn't look anything like the neighborhood we lived in. Inside the leather interior of our Ford I felt safe and protected. But I was disturbed. Why didn't they hate us? Why should we get to live like royalty while these people were just scraping by? These drives to and from the Polo Grounds were a history lesson, intended or not, which spawned a secular Jewish Liberal. Life clearly wasn't fair, as President John F. Kennedy would remind the nation a dozen years later and, although I didn't believe that I was in any way personally responsible for that circumstance, I felt guilty about it nevertheless. How was it possible that my own family could have suffered the effects of racial and economic injustice, while at the same time I could feel as privileged as I did during those drives through Harlem? I thought you were supposed to feel good if you were privileged. Perhaps there is such a thing as Jewish DNA.

One day, when I was still in the fourth grade, I came home from school with this question for my father: "Dad, some kids at school have started asking me what I am. You know, what religion? What should I tell them?"

"You tell them you're an American, like they are. Then you can tell them you're also a Jew."

As a young boy, it was hard *not* to see the world as an embattled place. I couldn't understand why the "have-nots" didn't just swarm across 96th Street and take whatever they wanted. The "have-nots" were stronger, more athletic, and lived lives full of hard knocks. They were just the opposite of me. Why didn't they act the way the angry masses did in the Hollywood movies I saw about the

French Revolution? How come we were so lucky?

I was lucky in other ways, too. My cousin, Everett Sloane, was a well-respected character actor during the forties and fifties and played Bernstein in *Citizen Kane* and Rita Hayworth's lawyer husband in *The Lady from Shanghai.* I was fascinated that he could change his accent from French to German to Italian, and so on. He could do any dialect called for by a script and would often launch into his own routines whenever he felt the impulse to entertain the people around him. He transformed himself into outsized characters at family gatherings and social occasions. It was difficult to know who he really was when he was just "being himself," but he was very entertaining. He was the perfect example of a "grownup" acting out. We were never really close, but I knew him as well as he'd let me, from birth until shortly before he intentionally swallowed too many sleeping pills and ended his life at the age of fifty-five.

I was also privileged to be told a lot of "inside scoop" about the goings on of movie-set life by Paul Stewart, my dad's boyhood friend from the Bronx. He was a well-known movie actor who played Kirk Douglas' fight manager in *Champion* and Roland, the butler, in *Citizen Kane*. He sounded like Bogart with a New York snarl in his voice and a street-smart swagger. He and Everett did a lot of radio work and were regulars on Orson Welles' *Mercury Theatre on the Air*, a weekly live broadcast that frightened the entire nation in 1938 when it presented *The War of the Worlds*. Welles deliberately left out the usual opening format that clarified to the listener that what followed was fiction, not fact. The program drew a squad of police officers to the studio, who were alarmed by the mass exodus it was causing in New Jersey where the Martians had supposedly landed an invading army.

When it came to the subject of "acting," Paul liked to keep things simple.

"Acting is just a lot of tricks," he opined. "An actor has to find little pieces of behavior to express how he feels. He may toss a hat on a chair or light a cigarette and blow smoke rings in the air. The important thing is to be natural."

This is why many actors report that they spend the first half of their careers learning how to act and the second half, learning how not to. Growing up, like a fly on the wall, I heard their unending frustrations about the business, although they both made a decent living by most standards and were considered successful. They wanted other people to think they were, anyway, and lived beyond their means on many occasions. But, having been born poor and survived the Great Depression, they felt they had the right to enjoy themselves when they were in the money. They were constantly concerned that there might not be a next job. And, even if there was, any job, no matter how good or monetarily remunerative, was destined to end. All shows close, movies "wrap," and programs go off the air. Even when the going was good, it never lasted.

It was at summer camp in New Hampshire at the age of twelve that my ability to perform became my salvation. Camp Winnaukee had a highly sports-oriented program committed to all sorts of competitive activities. Running faster than the next guy was not my strong suit, and when it came time to compete in the crowning event of the summer, the Color War Relay Race, my worst nightmare came true. I didn't volunteer for this event, but everyone was forced to participate. It was supposed to be good for you. As I rounded second base, I tripped and fell. My team on the sidelines went ballistic. The "boo's" and catcalls were merciless and as I staggered to my feet, a runner on the other team passed me easily on his way to home plate. It cost my team (which just happened to be half the camp) the lead, and they clearly didn't appreciate it. I was given the silent treatment for days. To atone for this disaster, I was offered the chance to recite a poem I'd never heard of called, *The Oracle of Delphi.* I had a strong voice, spoke clearly, and won the prize for that category. I was redeemed, and my running debacle was forgotten. It was forgotten until it was discovered that I had waged a bet that may own bunkmates would lose their final game of the camp basketball tournament, which they did. They viewed my having won my bet as a betrayal of "team spirit" and prevailed upon me to volunteer to represent my bunk in the All-Camp Boxing Tournament. I drew an opponent by the name of Edelman, whom I had never met. He towered over me with his long arms and huge shoulders. Each round was three minutes in length, and I never landed a single blow. I don't think I even raised my gloves. It was a catastrophe. For three rounds I was pummeled and chased around the ring. The only respite came when the referee came between us and momentarily provided a buffer against Edelman's onslaught, but during these brief interludes I made an amazing discovery: the more I reeled and stumbled, the more laughter I heard from the happy, jeering multitude surrounding me.

My counselors were having a particularly good time at my expense and the more I wobbled, the more they roared. It was a cheap way to get laughs, but it restored my sense of dignity and control. Instead of laughing *at* me, they were laughing *with* me, and that made all the difference. It was a lesson I would never forget.

About this time, I signed up for a neighborhood drama club which put on modest productions at the Hans Jaeger House, located in the middle of what was referred to as Germantown on East 85th Street. None of us knew it at the time, but there were frequent Bund meetings there during the war sponsored by neo-Nazi sympathizers. There were some rowdy types who came to see these plays from time to time, and one afternoon, upon making my first entrance, I was drenched to the bone by a couple of water pistol-toting semi-delinquents in the front row. What a shock! Making an entrance could be dangerous.

I really lucked out when I was given the lead in the eighth-grade graduation play at PS 6. We put on a staged adaptation of a radio play by Arthur Miller called *Grandpa and the Statue*, and I was Grandpa. The play was set at the base of the Statue of Liberty, where I explained the idea of America to my grandson. I walked with a cane and wore a beard glued on with the usual, foul-smelling spirit gum. I walked like an old man and squinted at the marble as I spoke the words,

"Give me your tired, your poor, your hungry masses yearning to breathe free..." It certainly made me think of Nachman Trochman.

I got high marks from the school janitor after the performance. He said I had the makings of a star, but if there was ever a next time, I should make sure that my fly was zipped up before I came onstage.

At this point in my development, I was privy to an extraordinary experience: I saw first hand the benefit that notoriety could bring.

"Get dressed," my father said as he woke me on a Saturday morning. I was thirteen. "We're going to the race track with Milton Berle and Mickey Rooney!" I got dressed in a hurry. The limousine picked us up an hour later, and I had the most riotous day of my life. Uncle Milty, as he was known to the rest of the world, had dated my mother when they were in high school. She said he always wanted to neck with her in a phone booth. They were dear friends now and he and his family came to my tenth birthday party. He was the biggest television star in the history of the medium having sold, according to RCA, more television sets than any other entertainer in history. I sure knew who Mickey Rooney was, but I had never met him. In the car they were both very "on" and ad-libbed in iambic pentameter all the way to Aqueduct Racetrack. They wrote songs, leaned out the window and hollered at people, and told stories using the dirtiest words I had ever heard. I was in pain from laughing. Milton's delivery was aggressive in a way that demanded that you laugh. He *lived* to get laughs, and would keep going until he got one. If Rooney took a pause from his own schtick, Milton would fill it in with a croak, or a fart, or spell a word using the wrong letters. It was brilliant. More amazing was that once we got to the track, everybody treated them as if they were old friends. There were endless handshakes and warm familiar greetings, sprinkled with wisecracks and good humored insults. Even in the men's room, everyone wanted to shake Milton's hand. It was obvious; being famous meant that everyone would want to be your friend.

The first professional acting class I ever took was at the Herbert-Berghof Studio in Greenwich Village when I was seventeen years-old. Anthony Manino was the acting teacher. He asked us to go up on the small stage at the front of the room and examine the floor. This was his assignment to the class: examine the floor. About ten of us wandered around the stage for a few minutes and stared at the old wooden floor boards. Then, one by one, we returned to our seats.

"Do any of you feel that you've examined the floor thoroughly?" he asked. This question was met with a stony silence. He continued, "Maybe that's because you didn't know *why* you were examining the floor. What if I told you that you were the stage manager of a ballet company and the Prima Ballerina had limped into the wings with a bloody toe after her final exit. Your job is to find out what caused it to happen. Now, how would you examine the floor? Show me."

Again, we rose and set about the task, but this time our inspection was different. We got on our hands and knees and ran our fingers over the surface of the wood. We felt for splinters or bits of glass until satisfied that we had completed our assignment. The lesson learned was that acting is "doing things, mentally and physically, with a purpose, and that doing so brings with it the ability to focus, along with a natural sense of relaxation." It was a good first lesson.

I also took a few classes from Bill Hicky, who I would appear with twenty years later on Broadway in *Arsenic and Old Lace*, and Myra Rostova, who was Montgomery Clift's mentor. I was learning the vocabulary that the pros used when they spoke about acting.

One of my earliest obsessions had to do with time itself, and the problems it posed. Everything was always changing and fading into the past. Perhaps I felt that way because I changed schools three times within a span of two years before I was ten. As I got older I felt compelled to visit my old haunts and take photographs as if it were a way to capture the past and create a sense of permanence. I wanted proof of the existence of things as well as proof that I had been there. I wanted to stop time, which always seemed to be hurtling me into new realities. Perhaps that's the real reason for this memoir as I try to capture the essence of who I was at various stages of my life.

During the summers before college I spent time at my family's summer cottage in Ocean Beach, Fire Island. Our house was a hangout for a loud and funny crowd of regulars, including Mel Brooks, Carl Reiner, Zero Mostel, Milton Berle, and others. I came home one night to discover about forty people sitting on the floor listening to Mel and Carl perform their *2000 Year-Old Man* routine before it was ever heard publicly.

I felt I was destined to be an actor. I loved the world of "make believe." Being surrounded by a lively group of outsized personalities, and having been exposed to the highest quality of theatre, I knew where I wanted to go. I had the advantage of a wise insider; my father. He was an anomaly of sorts in that his commitment to protect the working man by raising minimum wages, offering health insurance, and establishing pension plans for union workers, was a sharp contrast from his greatest wish for me; that I achieve the kind of success that would put me ahead of the pack. I remember when he professed that it wasn't worth a lot being a professional actor, unless one achieved stardom.

A few blocks from our summer home was the beach house that belonged to the most famous acting guru at the time, Lee Strasberg. I had become friends with his son, Johnny. I had a crush on his slightly older sister, Susan, who was already working as a professional actress. She used to borrow my bike, but had no time for me. She was out of my league. I passed out in the Strasberg's bathroom one evening after drinking too much wine at dinner. I still recall murmuring to myself as I lay on the floor, not aware that my feet were blocking the bathroom door: "Here I am in the home of the world's greatest acting teacher and I'm too dizzy to stand up. At least John Barrymore drank and could act. All I wanted to do was throw up!"

I recovered and the Strasberg's were very understanding. Lee could be very intimidating, even in the casual atmosphere of a summer beach house. I asked Paula, his wife, if he might have a moment to give me a little advice about my career. A few days later she led me up a rickety stairway to the upper deck. Lee was in a rocking chair gazing out at the ocean.

"You're asking me who is the finest acting teacher in America? I would say Alvina Krause at Northwestern University. It's a good place to start because you'll be in a lot of plays and get your stage legs. If you stay in the city, trying to make a living at the same time, you'll spend your days waiting on tables and hunting down auditions. Get comfortable first in front of people. You can learn the rest later."

It was the best advise I ever got. I was sixteen at the time and never had the chance to speak with him again, but I will always be grateful that he led me to Alvina Krause. She turned out to be the most inspiring and influential person in my life.

Alvina Krause

Alvina Krause was known all over the country by ambitious and talented "actor wannabe's." Northwestern University in Evanston, Illinois was turning out a disproportionate number of successful theatre people, and everybody knew it. The short list included Patricia Neal, Inga Swenson, Charlton Heston, Jeffery Hunter, Carol Lawrence, Walter Kerr, Martha Hyre, Paul Lynde, and many others.

Her great achievement was that she had the ability to expand horizons, to bring people to a sense of their own potential, to create a vision of what the theatre can be, but generally isn't. Some thought she trained us for a theatre that doesn't exist.

I was eighteen years-old and sitting in the dark in the last row of the large auditorium where the acting classes were held. Many of my classmates sat down front, to be near her—at her feet, so to speak. I didn't want to appear too idolatrous and resisted the temptation by taking a seat back in Row W.

There were two students performing a scene on stage. I judged their efforts and arrived at my own conclusions. My thoughts were private, of course. There was no one anywhere near me. And then, suddenly, over the heads of the believers in the first row, Miss Krause, in the middle of her critique, which seemed uncannily like mine, craned her head and focused her eyes into the dark where I sat. Once having found me, she said, "I'm right, aren't I, Roberts?" I was stunned. A few moments later the class ended, but I sat down front, as close as I could get, from that day on.

She was rather short with sharp features and wore her hair in a bun. Her voice was thin, yet commanding, but it was her eyes that gave her a quality that can only be described as supernatural. They looked into your soul. She was someone on a holy crusade and was often referred to as "God" by her students. She had an inspired flair for the dramatic gesture. Pacing back and forth between the stage and the first row of seats, she often waved a purple handkerchief in the air to punctuate her points. "The purpose of acting," she said, after a suspenseful pause, "is to illuminate and enlighten. The theatre is the last, best chance to save the world."

And she meant it. She would stare at the floor with a squint, her arms folded across her chest while she conjured her next thoughts. "All that is needed to find the truth in any situation, or in any character, is to closely observe human behavior and apply your imagination."

One of her earliest assignments was to study an animal of our choice at the zoo, and bring it credibly to life in front of the class for a few moments. I chose to be a Blue-Tailed Skink, a slithery reptile without much personality. I can still do my skink, although it's a little rough on the torso. She wanted us to make up stories in our heads, as if filling in the blanks of a script, which she described as being a map without pictures. She said, "An actor must be a little more and a little better than anyone else. He must be able to play a genius today and a fool tomorrow, and understand both, to have a voice which is strong, flexible, and controlled. To have a body which responds to command and which can handle a renaissance rapier or a cowboy's lariat, if need be. He must know something of music, art, and a great deal of life. His senses must be sharper than anyone else's. He must be able to perceive the world as a king perceives it, or a saint, or a stevedore. He must know all places and all times, for he may be called upon to play them."

Miss Krause could sometimes become impatient. She had the ability to inspire those she believed had talent, which another great acting teacher, Stella Adler, defined as "the ability to learn," but she could also be dismissive of those she didn't. She would often interrupt a student's entrance. "Cut! Flunk!" she would holler out before any dialogue had even been spoken. "Where were you coming from? Why did you come into this space? What is your purpose? Come in again, and this time make me know where you just came from and why you're here!"

At regular intervals during the school year, she preached her doctrine in a venue called "Workshop Theatre," which consisted of three one-act presentations with different casts and assigned directors. Alvina Krause was at her most dazzling. After the curtain fell she would pace the aisles praising, or damning, as she went. Praise from her might mean that an up-and-coming freshman would be in-demand next semester for a major production, but a verbal drubbing in front of the entire theatre department could also leave lasting scars.

I spent two summers at her Playhouse in Eaglesmere, Pennsylvania. It was a perfect arena for the application of her theories. There, we put on plays in a rustic, converted barn nestled among the trees near the shore of a quiet mountain lake.

Eight plays enjoyed a one-week run during July and August for a mostly subscription audience made up of locals and guests from the quaint hotels surrounding the area. Sets were built and costumes made by all of us in the company, twenty-five of her favorite students from the Northwestern campus, and a few from Yale. We lived together in a three-story house with white shingles and shared meals three times a day.

There was a small tuition fee, but if you agreed to work in the kitchen, that could be waived. There were no drugs, hardly any alcohol, and a few summer romances. We were constantly exhausted and had the best time of our lives.

"What is the play about?" she would ask. She insisted that we discuss the entire play before we tried to "act" anything. "What is the theme of the play? What idea does the author implant? How does the character you're cast as advance the theme of the play?"

Answering these questions, after thoughtful deliberation, stimulated our imaginations. It also gave us a road map intended to keep us from getting lost.

She insisted that we become aware of the context in which great plays were written and why. What follows is a brief syllabus, condensed from four years of study, defining the styles and purposes of theatre throughout the ages.

The Greeks dealt with big ideas about fate and destiny (*Oedipus Rex, Antigone, Media, The Trojan Women, The Orestia*). The actors wore masks to represent the characters and had to project their speeches in large outdoor arenas.

The Roman theatre was diminished in the eyes of theatre historians because it put its emphasis on spectacle rather than on ideas.

The dark ages, pre-Renaissance, didn't produce much theatre worth saving until Shakespeare who, as if by a miracle, wrote about everything and everybody. He wrote comedies, histories, tragedies, et al.

The French wrote satires about the rich and aimed their critical tongues at the hypocrisies of the age. Molière used farce to make his points.

In Russia, Chekov began writing plays about real people whose problems and circumstances reflected those of the upper middle class a few decades before the Communist Revolution of 1917.

In Norway, Henrik Ibsen would write important social and political plays about injustice and would alter the role of women in the world forever through the creation of the world's first liberated woman: Nora in *A Doll's House.*

In England, George Bernard Shaw would castigate the status quo of his culture in many plays on many subjects. He also invented Eliza Doolittle, another liberated woman, who became the modern *Pygmalion* in *My Fair Lady*.

In America it was Eugene O'Neill who wrote about the dreams of dreamers, immigrants, farmers, poets, seamen, and some think the seminal play about family and the American dream: *Long Day's Journey Into Night*.

In Germany, Bertold Brecht was so intent on getting people involved against fascism that he invented a new kind of theatre that used circus acts and musical interludes to prevent the audience from becoming sentimental about his causes. He wanted to force them to think about the consequences of their inattention to what was going on in the streets of Berlin in 1935.

On the Lower East Side of Manhattan, at the beginning of the 20th Century, a group of immigrant exiles from the Ukraine had established what was known as the Yiddish Theatre, which combined the folkish humor of Sholem Alechem, a short-story writer with

English Music Hall tradition and Vaudeville clowning thrown in. This gave birth to the form known today as musical comedy.

Then the naturalists, or behaviorists, came along and focused on Freudian motivational theories to explore complex characters created by the likes of Clifford Odets, William Inge, Tennessee Williams, and Arthur Miller. Thus, we get *Golden Boy, A Streetcar Named Desire, The Glass Menagerie, Picnic, The Crucible,* and *Death of a Salesman.*

With the rise of Darwinism and existentialism, the next frontier for the theatre was led by the Absurdists in the 1950s including Beckett, Ionesco, Albee, and Pinter. We got *Waiting for Godot, The Bald Soprano, The Zoo Story,* and *The Homecoming.*

The staple of the commercial theatre for decades in the West End and on Broadway has been the light boulevard comedy of manners represented best by Richard Brinkley Sheridan, Noël Coward, George S. Kaufman, S.N. Berman, and Neil Simon.

On the lawn, in front of the theatre not far from the box office, a group of us would begin to rehearse our lines before working in the actual theatre. Another play was being staged there. At night, the house was full as a paying audience watched a third play. It was a round-robin arrangement.

If I wasn't cast in a production, I was expected to report to either the scenery or costume shops and put in my time. The scenery shop was in a swelteringly hot shed on the premises, filled with machinery, saws, sawdust, and hard labor. I preferred the costume shop because it was in a cool barn and they always had some good music coming out of the radio. I couldn't really sew, but most of the girls could, and that's where they were.

Miss Krause would roam the grounds and contribute her wisdom as she felt inspired to. We could sense her whereabouts as courtiers could sense the whereabouts of royalty in the Shakespeare plays we put on. At times she was cold, angry, demanding, and brutally honest, or she might be coy, playful, and girlish. A student once wrote this about her:

> "I was coming down the walk from the library toward Foster Street and I saw this adorable little girl running down the sidewalk in her Overalls. I had to just stop and watch her. She was so peppy and bright-eyed, and she was having so much fun just running down the street. Then she got to the corner, and I realized it wasn't a little girl. It was Alvina Krause in her slacks, hurrying to drop a letter in the mailbox."

I was particularly fond of the tennis ball exercise she would have us employ, when the ideas of a play weren't being tossed out to the audience in a compelling way. One of us would stand at the back row of the theatre and have an actual catch with another actor on the stage. You were supposed to throw the ball on the active verb of your sentence and be prepared to catch it and its meaning when it was thrown back.

In another illustration of her resourcefulness, during a rehearsal of Friedrich Dürrenmatt's *The Visit*, she brought to life a scene in which the townspeople of a squalid Eastern European village discuss the fate of the protagonist Anton Schill. His life hangs in the balance as they debate whether or not to turn him over to his executioner. His death would be repaid with a hefty ransom. Alvina Krause mounted the stage and ordered that all the lights in the theatre be turned off. She instructed the actors, now in pitch black, to continue with the lines of the scene, and lurked among them in the dark, whispering softly into their ears what they had at stake, what they could win, or lose, according to the outcome.

"Wouldn't you like a new barn?" she said conspiratorially. Or, "Couldn't you use a warm coat for the coming winter, or a better plow for the field?" Gradually, the actors withdrew into their own reflections and private thoughts.

Then, suddenly, she turned on all the lights. "Look at each other," she demanded. "What is your neighbor thinking? Are you proud of your own thoughts, or are you ashamed? Which of you will be the first to take the life of Anton Schill?" In this way she elicited a sense of suspicion, paranoia, and community evil, which convinced us it was the idea the playwright had in mind all along.

When the words were too easily spoken or uninvested, she would suggest saying the lines in a foreign language, even if you didn't speak it well. The struggle to do this forced the imagination, and the body, to find different modes of expression. "Character creation starts with the spine," she'd preach. "Find one in a person you can observe and recreate it, mimic it, and mirror it. It's the best place to start when creating a character."

I was onstage rehearsing a scene from Schiller's *Mary Stuart* when Ms. Krause decided to "expand my horizons," as was her wont.

"You've got to experience the emotion of panic that the character you're playing must be feeling at this point in the play." she said from the third row of the theatre.

The character I was playing had just been found out to be a traitor. He is alone for a moment, somewhere in a castle, talking out loud to himself about his available escape options. There aren't many, as his allies are already in retreat.

"You can't just say the words." As Ms. Krause said this, she advanced toward the stairs that led to the stage. As quick as a flash, she stood a foot away from me as I continued to say my lines. Suddenly, I felt her flat open hand swipe across my cheek along with the sting that came with it.

"Keep going!" she said. I did, and so did she. She struck me on my other cheek. Instinctively, I began to back up until my heels hit the two-foot-high platform that comprised the upstage level of the set, but Alvina Krause was still pummeling. I decided to avoid further punishment and stepped gingerly up on to the riser becoming finally out of her reach, or so I thought. Ever so resourceful, Ms. Krause grabbed a nearby chair, placed it in front of the platform where I stood, and stood on it in order to continue her onslaught. I was trapped, flustered, perspiring, and truly frightened. Apparently, it showed, because she ended the "exercise" by climbing down off the chair and saying, "That's more like it.

Hang on to that idea and don't forget it!" Obviously, I never have.

All of us at Eaglesmere knew we were in the presence of genius. She had no family of her own, but her students became her family. We felt. and were right to feel, that we were a privileged band of players unlikely to ever find a mind as keen as hers again.

I made sure to keep in touch with her after I graduated. She came to New York once or twice and saw me on Broadway. Like a visiting aunt from another time and place, she was shy and unassuming.

Fame was never her idol—teaching was. She died in 1984 at the age of eighty-two. They named a theatre after her in Bloomsberg, Pennsylvania, where she spent her last years, and it still survives today.

In one of the few interviews she gave, a journalist asked her to define the most necessary quality for an actor to possess if he were to succeed in his career. She paused to contemplate this and then answered with one word, "Belief."

Whether she meant the ability to believe in a fictionalized set of circumstances that provoke real thoughts and feelings, or whether she meant an actor's belief in the transformative power of theatre itself, I have never been sure. I think she may have meant both. At any rate, her faith in her students was transforming all by itself. She nurtured us as if we were part of her well-tended garden, and many of us flowered because of her driven belief that teaching was her purpose on Earth.

The idealistic foundation wasn't always accepted by my elder mentors in the business. They ascribed the purpose of commercial theatre to be purely monetary, and they found my zealotry naïve. I left Northwestern University with a fervor to fulfill her vision of a theatre bringing catharsis in a way that sent an audience out into the world more enlightened than they were when they came in. The theatre was not just meant to entertain. It sprang from a noble cause and, for the first time in my life, I felt stirred as if by some religious idealism.

On one of my last days in Evanston, Illinois, I chose to sit out on one of the long piers that jut out into Lake Michigan. I'd been on that pier before, when I tried to persuade another classmate to return to shore and forgive the drama teacher who had harshly criticized her an hour earlier. It was mid-February at the time and under the pier, where she stood, the water was waist deep. Actresses, as you may have heard, can be very bull-headed sometimes, but she eventually trudged out of the water and went back to class.

Now, near graduation, I was out on the end of that pier, with water on three sides, looking back towards the campus that had been my home for four years. I went out there to be alone and steel myself for the next big thing: the future. Was I going to make it? Would I be a success?

I wasn't sure what "make it" meant, specifically. I knew it meant making a living at the very least, but did it also mean becoming a great classical actor, like Laurence Olivier, my boyhood idol? Or, did it mean just making a living? I had done well enough against the competition at Northwestern, and they truly were a promising group of students, so I felt that the odds for success were in my favor. I also knew that I was already ahead of most of them because I had a family in New York City to live with as I got started. I didn't have to rent a room, or shop for dinner. For two years I lived at home. I also had the advantage of being given sound and experienced advice whenever I needed it. That came almost exclusively from my father who, despite his early reservations about my aspirations, had become such an enthusiast about it that I often felt I was groomed to become a success.

I made a conscious promise to myself on that pier. I promised never to quit, regardless of how discouraged I might become in the future. I would not betray my ambition. There was really nothing else in the world I wanted to do. I don't believe it was stardom that inspired me. That seemed too far away to think about and too unknown to relate to, but I had the necessary confidence to believe that I could be a working actor; someone respected by his peers like my cousin Everett, or my dad's best friend Paul Stewart. They struggled with early poverty (which I never did) and they survived the Blacklist (which I never had to face), but they threw themselves into their work and fought to stay in their field. I was determined not to fail, not only for myself, but in some way for them, too. Perhaps, most of all, for my father.

I spent a week in Berlin after graduation, inspired by what I was convinced was the most activist political use of "theatre" at that time. The style developed by the Brecht Berliner Ensemble was on display at the theatre he founded in East Berlin. It deconstructed the elements of traditional "theatre reality" and forced the audience to reject sentimentality in exchange for reasoned ideas. I couldn't speak a word of German, but I had read the play I was about to see, *The Rise and Fall of the Third Reich.* It used all the tools of drama and stagecraft to expose the villainy of the Nazi era. This was the kind of theatre Alvina Krause believed could change the world for the better. I rode a rented bicycle through the Brandenburg Gate to East Berlin at dusk, just six weeks before the construction of the Berlin Wall. I enjoyed every moment of the production I saw, and I liked pedaling out after dark just as much.

I was determined to make a structured and disciplined approach to the task of becoming a success. I didn't have to be as transformative an actor as the hero of my generation, Marlon Brando, but I had to make a living. This meant taking advantage of any opportunity that might come my way. They didn't all turn out well. It's ironic that despite my fondness for Stuart Little, one of my first professional jobs was to play the theatrical agent of a small mouse named Topo Gigio, the star of a regular novelty act on *The Ed Sullivan Show*. I was flown to Pinewood Studios in London where the pilot episode was shot at Sullivan's expense. His son-in-law was the producer. The twelve-inch-tall mouse and I sang a duet of *Singin' in the Rain* as we travelled in a Pullman car to our next scheduled vaudeville performance. Three Italian puppeteers, who spoke no English, worked the tiny instruments that manipulated the hands and legs of Topo as we performed our choreography. I liked being twenty-one in London and sitting a table away from John Wayne in the commissary, but the project was perceived, by the powers that be, to be a disaster and was never heard of again.

It seems that despite wanting to match the valor and courage displayed by Laurence Olivier's Henry V and admiring the guts displayed by Burt Lancaster in a host of roles, the truth is that early in my career I danced with a midget mouse, was run over by a herd of ducks in my first film, and later, in *Popcorn*, mortally stabbed through the chest by a giant mosquito. As the old adage goes, "Life is what happens while you're making other plans."

At any rate, I left college determined to make a living as an actor but also determined, if I had the chance, to take Alvina Krause's principles seriously. The time had come for me to face "the business."

The Business

"You know the five stages of an actor's career, don't you kid?"

I had a small part in a failed Broadway enterprise. We ran for two weeks. I was being addressed by one of the soon to be out of work members of the cast.

"No. What are they?" I asked. We were waiting in the wings for the curtain to go up at the Belasco Theatre on West 44th Street.

"Phase One: Who's Tony Roberts?"
"Phase Two: Get me Tony Roberts!"
"Phase Three: Get me a Tony Roberts type!!"
"Phase Four: Get me a young Tony Roberts!"
"Phase Five: Who's Tony Roberts?"

These phases form a familiar template for most career arcs in show business. It was the first of several cynical attitudes I became accustomed to hearing from seasoned veterans.

"Be nice to the people you work with on the way up, because you're sure to meet them on the way down!"

"Kid, you need to have faith that when you're in a valley, there's going to be a hill up ahead. And when you're on that hill you can also be sure that there's a valley coming."

These homilies, though spoken ruefully, were meant to express sympathy for all those who have traveled this journey and seen the world from its various vantage points.

My father used to raise the blinds in my room when I was living at home after college and tell me it was time to hit the streets. I would wear a jacket and tie, gather my photos and résumés, and set out to make the rounds (meet and greet as many producers, casting directors, and agents as I could). I kept a file box filled with the names and addresses of everyone I had ever met who might give me a job and found ways to let them know I was alive, without becoming a pest or a stalker. Everyone thinks you're crazy to go into this business anyway, so you have to prove that you're in it for the long haul. It may take two years just to convince a casting director that you can be trusted to show up on opening night.

My father said, "Consider the postage stamp, my son. It sticks to one thing until it gets there!" He also stressed two contradicting philosophies. On one hand he had tremendous sympathy for those he referred to as "working actors," meaning anybody who didn't get star billing. These were the people who always had to audition for roles, were paid mostly at union scale, and never knew where their next meal was coming from. On the other hand, he made it clear that my ambition should be aimed at becoming a star because unless I was, I would never achieve the peace of mind or financial security that had eluded so many of his contemporaries.

Dad said, "Stars get to be stars because they have great personalities." It stayed in my head and now sounds like something Willy Loman might have said. One of the most frequently repeated bits of advice I was given by my father was not to celebrate a promising turn of events before there was concrete evidence that it was warranted.

"Did you sign the contract?" he would ask. This was always a preface to the pouring of champagne. Otherwise, a good deal of energy might be wasted explaining the turn of events which had not worked out in my favor. It was always safer to wait until things were officially legal. He even suggested that the best "post-audition" state of mind was one of forgetfulness. Why waste time worrying if they liked you or not? If they did and you were offered the job, then that was the time to call your friends and spread the word. If they didn't want you, it was not worth one moment of your time stewing about it. Eventually, I developed a thick skin to the rejections and disappointments the business handed out. Being under-appreciated came with the territory and if you couldn't handle it, then maybe you were in the wrong profession. I was tutored to expect tough odds, but also taught the best strategy to overcome them: persistence and dogged perseverance. My father thought the way to get ahead was pounding the pavement and, even when I got a job, he implored me to take advantage of it in every way I could until it was replaced by another one. The job itself was the reward and the "fun" part. It was getting the job that was the hard work. I have learned nothing in the fifty years since to dispute that conclusion.

After college, I did what most actors do when they're starting out, which meant that I took whatever job I could get. I did some summer stock in Westport, Connecticut, and I auditioned for whatever I could find through information in the trade papers such as *Backstage* and *Show Business.* Thanks to the *Ross Reports*, available at local newsstands, I was up to date on who the casting agents were and where they were located. I replaced an actor in an Off-Broadway musical that had been running for some time and collected unemployment insurance, twice exhausting my available limit. I think the amount was thirty-five dollars a week for six months and then it expired. I did an "under five" role on *The Edge of Night*, a daytime soap opera that was aired live (An "under five" role is one with few lines to say—under five—and automatically puts you in a separate category, so they don't have to pay you as much). It was a first step on the soap opera ladder. If you were congenial, on-time, and did what you were told without any fuss, you were a good candidate for a larger role in the future.

Larry Hagman, later to be a star on *Dallas*, was the star of *The Edge of Night.* I was playing an airline clerk. It was my debut. His first line as my customer was, "Is the two o'clock flight from Chicago on time?"

Now it was my turn. I waited until his eyes lifted from his script, took a deep breath, adjusted the cap I had brought from home, gazed into his eyes intently and said, as earnestly as I could, "No, sir. That plane is going to be a little late."

Silence. Larry Hagman froze in amazement. His jaw fell open. At last he found his voice and said, not in an unkind way, but with honest sincerity, "You're not going to *act*, are you?" as if I had committed a cardinal sin.

Everyone present had a laugh on the "new boy" and the director insisted that I join him for lunch before the broadcast. Lunch was in the bar across the street, and the drinks were on him. It was part of my initiation, he said as he ordered me a shot or two of his favorite blend. His name was Dick Sandwick and I would meet him again a year later when I was cast as Lee Pollock on *The Edge of Night.*

Being a regular on a soap is like being adopted by two families at the same time. One is the family of characters who live in the fictional world created by the writers, and the other family are the actors, cameramen, make-up artists, wardrobe personnel, etc. with whom you may interact for years. In the 1960s most of the soaps were broadcast live, so there was no chance to get something right the second time. As a result, there was a certain pressure on everybody to come to work prepared. The make-up room before the first camera run-through of the day was the place to be; the height of the party, so to speak. That's where gossip flourished, good-natured ribbing was welcome, egos were scoffed at, and best of all, the network biggies weren't there and they took a beating. It was a chance to frolic before facing the music on live television.

Eventually I played the recurring role of Lee Pollack. Lee was an architect and confined to a wheelchair most of the time. It made the blocking easy. I met a lot of wonderful actors and learned to relax in front of the camera.

I discovered that each day the cast would indulge in what amounted to an unacknowledged challenge match. They would straggle into the morning rehearsals slightly bleary eyed, scripts in hand, coffee cups at the ready, and dish about whatever they had done the night before. The last thing they wanted to do was to take the script seriously. Any irreverence towards the material was welcomed by all, and few jokes were off limits. The trick was to be so diffident and blithe about the task at hand that cast and crew alike would wonder at the magic of your own transformation when the time came. It was like saying, "I can rehearse less than you and still be sharp!" The first time any "acting" showed up was later in the day, after lunch, when it came time for the final dress rehearsal. In many ways it was a great gift because, coming when it did, there was a freshness to it that prompted credible reactions from other actors who, until this moment, hadn't really been listening to anything anybody said.

Sandwick played a prank on the entire company that outranked all others. Pollack, my character, suffered from a life-threatening illness and I was required to lay comatose in a hospital bed for several days. *The Edge of Night* went on the air every afternoon at 3:30pm. On this particular day, Sandwick received a phone call shortly after lunch from a network executive informing him that a Presidential news conference had been announced. The show would be pre-empted that afternoon and there would be no broadcast. Sandwick asked if he could dismiss the cast, but the executive insisted the show be prepared as usual.

"Why?" asked Sandwick.

"Well, there might be an assassination or something," came the reply.

"Oh, sure, I can hear it now. 'Due to the assassination of the President, we now bring you *The Edge of Night*!'" offered Sandwick.

"Well, you've got to rehearse until airtime, anyway," said the executive and hung up.

The cast greeted this news with a groan and resigned itself to stay until officially released. We rehearsed, but lackadaisically. Mostly, we sat around and twiddled our thumbs.

At twenty-five minutes past three, the cast and crew assembled around the monitors in the studio expecting to see the last few minutes of the scheduled three o'clock program, and then the President appear on the screen. Some of us even had our hats and coats on. Suddenly, the monitors all went blank. Then came the announcement from the control room. It was Sandwick and he was frantic.

"Jesus," he said over the loudspeaker, "I can't believe it! We're going on! We're on in two minutes! Two minutes, everybody! Places! Places! Jesus!"

Pandemonium ensued. People scattered in every direction looking for scripts, rewinding teleprompters, getting into costumes, slapping on make-up, wheeling cameras around, you name it: CHAOS.

"One minute, everybody! One minute to air!" Sandwick screamed.

I ran to the hospital room set, climbed onto the bed and got under the covers. I had an easy part because I had no dialogue, but the other actors could be heard swearing and praying as they tried to memorize lines they never thought they'd have to say.

"TEN SECONDS, PEOPLE! TEN SECONDS TO AIR!"

Mine was the opening scene. The camera would reveal me as I lay on my back and then pan to the door as my grieving mother would enter, having come to keep vigil by my bedside.

The organ sounded the opening theme of *The Edge of Night* and the stage manager waved his script under one of the cameras to signal that we were, in fact, on the air.

But it wasn't my mother who opened the door. It was Sandwick wearing a babushka! He burst in with his arms flung wide and shrieked with glee, "Bubby, you're not dead!" and threw himself on the bed in a fit of hysterics. For a moment, everyone in the studio froze. As it dawned on us that we had been misled to believe that we would be on the air, we all erupted with boisterous laughter to his masterful prank. What followed was a unified urge to strangle Sandwick. He had conned an entire cast and crew. He had a brilliant practical joker's imagination. The Presidential news conference had been put on, but we were the ones who were really put on, even if we never were, if you know what I mean.

My early career was full of ups and downs. There were auditions won, but more often auditions that went nowhere. I auditioned for commercials, voice overs, soap operas, and summer stock. I was a panelist on daytime game shows and played small parts on the TV shows that were produced in New York. I even played a dead body in the opening scene of *The Defenders*, a popular series in the 1960s.

On a good day, I could get thrown out of at least half a dozen offices. I would chat with the receptionist, hand over my headshot and résumé, made up of mostly college credits, and add the new contact's name and address to my file. When there was anything to blow my horn over, I made sure these people were up to date.

When I was twenty-three, I had a real, old-fashioned screen test. I was flown to Hollywood where I was fitted, rehearsed, made-up, and finally led into a soundstage the size of an airplane hanger. There, in a small corner of the vast space, thirty or forty stagehands huddled on the edge of a bright circle of light. The light illuminated a little set replicating a booth in a coffee shop.

Once inside that circle of light, I felt as if I was alone with my fellow actor. The presence of the grips and technicians whose task it was to make the actors look good was negligible. Even the camera was hard to find. The table was set with real knives, forks, napkins, and a sugar bowl. Actual hot coffee was set before us. An intimate atmosphere was created. When the test was over, I felt that I had been given a fair chance to bring my talent to the proceedings.

That's not the way they do things anymore. Nowadays, there might be ten people in an office for an audition, plus a video camera to tape the proceedings for later viewing by other casting agents or producers for some future project. These auditions are not memorized, and they demand a performance without giving an actor the chance to develop one through the rehearsal process. There isn't even a script. There are just "sides," as they are called, two or three pages of dialogue lifted from the script. The other lines in the scene are read off-camera by someone you've probably never met.

I've never met an actor who could tell me that they knew how to best prepare for an audition. Sometimes I've memorized a scene and won the job. On the other hand, sometimes no prep is the best prep because something unanticipated may occur and reveal more of yourself than you could have ever hoped for. If you do memorize the scene, it's a good idea to hold the pages in your hand anyway, or you will be judged as if you are giving a full performance. It's a lot of guesswork because even *they* rarely know what they are looking for, and there's not too much you can do if you're too short, too fat, too old, or not ethnically appropriate.

Some actors will try anything to get the part. There's a showbiz joke about an actor who cut off his leg in order to win the role of Long John Silver in a stage production of *Treasure Island.* When he got to the audition, he was met by a shout from the rear of the auditorium, "Sorry! Wrong leg!"

Then there's the actress who auditioned all over town for years without getting anywhere, and was finally told she had landed a part. "Oh," she said sweetly. "I don't do parts. I only do auditions."

No amount of preparation for an audition can prepare an actor for the unexpected disaster. Karen Black, an ex-classmate of mine from Northwestern had an audition at the Biltmore Theatre during the early years of her career. After reading the scene aloud onstage, they asked if she'd mind hanging around to read again later. They directed her to a lounge on the balcony level where she could pass the time. Unfortunately, being a bit nearsighted, she opened a door and stepped out into bright sunshine. As the door shut irrevocably behind her, she discovered she was standing on top of the marquee with no way to get back inside or down. Eventually, the fire department came and rescued her with a ladder. She got the part.

I had the opportunity to watch auditions from the other side of the footlights when I wore my director's hat for *One of the All-Time Greats* by Charles Grodin. I hated the awkward introductions, and the even more uncomfortable moment after the reading when an actor would attempt a graceful exit without letting on that he desperately wanted some positive feedback, but that's more than one can expect at most auditions.

I was amazed at how poorly most of my peers presented themselves. They handled the social aspects well enough, but most of them succeeded in demonstrating only their ability to read lines and make them sound believable. There's nothing wrong with that, except that after three actors have read the same lines for you, it's impossible not to get bored listening to them.

At last, an actor performed a dumb show of his own devising which spoke volumes before he ever uttered a word from the script. He began by pretending to enter a restaurant where the scene was set. He opened an imaginary door upstage, peered in furtively, then crossed to a chair and slowly unbuttoned his topcoat. As he looked around, it was clear that he had invented a story for himself and what he did without saying a word was more real in its depiction of an actual person than anything anybody else had come close to creating.

A good audition is one in which the actor finds a way to bring some real piece of himself to the proceedings. The lines don't matter. Those doing the hiring have heard the lines before. What they need is a human being of flesh and blood to play the part.

The best acting is seamless and doesn't look like acting; it seems real. An audition is a performance that has to be given before the rehearsals have taken place, and before the actor can keep his acting from showing.

My first job on Broadway resulted from an audition I gave for Dore Schary and the Theatre Guild. I got a small part in a play, starring Sal Mineo, Ralph Meeker, and Kevin McCarthy, called *Something About a Soldier.* When I went to join Actors' Equity Association, I had to change my name from David Roberts because they already had a person by that name in the union. Legally I could have kept it because it was the name on my birth certificate and that takes precedence over any union, or corporation that might insist that it be changed. I didn't know that at the time and decided in the interests of expediency to call myself Anthony Roberts. Anthony was chosen by my parents to be my legal middle name, although I have never understood why. Anthony was supposedly their first choice, but since I was born with very fair skin, bright blond hair, and blue eyes they deemed Anthony, the name of a beloved cousin and the family doctor to be the wrong choice. David became the favored alternate. I looked more like an albino as a kid than an Italian stallion. Anthony was fine for the first decade of my career, but the Disney studio in Los Angeles was convinced by their research into names that I would fare much better as

Tony rather than Anthony because according to them it was easier to remember and friendlier.

Something About a Soldier opened out of town and only ran for two weeks at the Ambassador Theatre on West 49th Street, the smallest grossing house in the neighborhood at the time.

Dore was an old-fashioned gentleman in every respect. His manner was soft-spoken and his wardrobe immaculate. He could have been the head of General Motors. In fact, he had been the head of MGM and produced some fine movies in Hollywood including *Bad Day at Black Rock* and *Boys Town.* His pictures always had themes calling for social justice. *Something About a Soldier* was about a pacifist.

I was in a scene in the second act that took place on a moving train. We all had to jostle ourselves to make it seem credible. I played an air cadet who becomes wrongly handcuffed by a drunken sergeant to an army trainee on his way to the stockade. I was obviously about to miss my stop and was riled up about it. On opening night, Ralph Meeker, playing the sergeant, perhaps to soothe his nerves, indulged in a little too much vino himself and said the final line of the scene immediately after his entrance; thus, effectively cutting out my only two pages of dialogue. I couldn't allow this to happen in front of the New York Times critic, not to mention my parents, so I repeated my own first line until he realized his mistake and corrected it. After the curtain came down, Dore told me I had saved the show. "You were like a fire engine out there, kid. You wouldn't quit. You put out the fire!"

Perhaps, but the play received poor notices, and I was soon out of a job. Sam Wanamaker was a pal of my dad's, an old pro who became the resuscitator of the Old Globe Theatre in London. At the party at Sardi's after the opening of *Soldier*, when the reviews were in, Sam told me that I was "lucky" to be in a flop. He counseled me to stay out of a hit as long as I could:

> "Each time an actor works, he meets more people and becomes known to other producers and directors. His own work improves as well because

> of his exposure to other actors and their particular talents. If a show runs a long time, you may stop growing. You may get comfortable with the money. You may even need the money to sustain your new lifestyle. I say, keep your overhead low and learn as much as you can."

Having a Broadway credit, even one as short lived as *Something About a Soldier* gave me a legitimate claim to be considered more seriously by casting directors for future projects. A few weeks later, a casting director sent me to a television studio where auditions were being held for the title role in a new CBS pilot called *Howie* to be filmed in Los Angeles. There were several other actors there and our auditions were taped so that the "powers that be" could make an informed choice as to who would play *Howie*. The next evening, while I was having dinner with my parents, my mother answered the telephone and handed it to me. "It's Peter Lawford," she said. As far as I knew, no one in my family had any connection to Peter Lawford, and neither did

I. "He's calling from The White House." Lawford was one of the producers of *Howie* and he spent a lot of time with his in-laws, who happened to include the then-President of the United States, John F. Kennedy.

"Congratulations, Anthony." He certainly sounded like Peter Lawford. "We're delighted that you're going to be our Howie. Who should we call?"

"Thank you," I replied. "Call for what?"

"Who's your agent, kid? We're ready to make a deal!"

"Oh," I was stumped. "Gee, can I call you back in a few minutes?"

I didn't have an agent at this point, but my father had a suggestion. It's not often that an actor can approach an agency with a job offer in hand, so why not aim for the top? I put The White House on hold for the night, and the next morning I asked the Music Corporation of America (MCA), the most powerful television and film agency in the business at the time, to negotiate for me. Within twenty-four hours I had signed a seven-year contract with Desi-Lu Productions to play Howie, and had a three-year deal with MCA to represent me in all fields. Everything was happening so fast. The very next morning I flew to Los Angeles for my first taste of Hollywood and was met at the airport by my new agent in a cream-colored Cadillac convertible. As we drove away from LAX the sun was shining, the top was down, and I felt as if I'd arrived!

In fact, that's all I had done, despite having been assigned my own parking space on the Desi-Lu lot, where *I Love Lucy* and other staples of the culture were produced. I discovered that a parking space is an item as fiercely bargained for as a decent salary, or respectable billing, or the length of a commitment. I enjoyed the parking space for all of three days.

Howie was the story of a man, played by Paul Lynde of *Bye, Bye, Birdie* fame, who is driven to distraction by his infuriating son-in-law, played by me. In *Bye, Bye, Birdie*, Lynde hilariously depicted the frustrations that come with being the father of a teenaged daughter. I was a big fan. His trademark was to bring an over-the-top sense of hysteria to whatever part he played. It was only natural that I would find his faces and gestures amusing. Unfortunately, I found them too amusing and couldn't get a grip on myself. I would lie awake at night inventing ways to control my laughter when he said his lines. He wasn't trying to break me up, but the more he invested himself in his performance, the more helplessly I cracked up. I tried imagining scenes of death and suffering while he spoke, but nothing helped. The director seemed upset with me for other reasons.

"Listen, kid. You're not doing what we saw on your screen test. I'll show it to you." But he never did.

During those first two days on the set, I could sense that I wasn't hitting any home-runs. The director kept trying to enlarge my reactions to things. He wanted bigger faces from me. Nothing I did seemed to please him.

At five o'clock the next morning, the phone rang.

"Good morning," a woman said pleasantly. "Your director would like to meet with you at the studio in two hours. Can you be there?"

"Sure. Is anything wrong?" I said, trying to sound as if I'd been up for hours, but that was all she would tell me.

I drove to the lot and parked in my very own space for what would turn out to be the last time. I was surprised to find that my agent was there at that hour with his Cadillac and a cup of coffee for me in a cardboard cup. "What's up?" I asked, and was quickly ushered into a nearby office.

The director said that casting me to play Howie was a big mistake on his part and that the studio had decided "to go in a different direction." They wanted a broader and goofier version of Howie than the one I offered.

I was stunned and responded with disbelief. "You mean…I'm fired?" I half-laughed. I was more embarrassed than hurt at that point. The real feelings would come later.

"Don't take it badly. We just made a mistake, that's all. You're a good actor and you're going to have a swell career."

Back in the parking lot, the agent from MCA said, "If you ask my advice, you'll get out of town before this story follows you around. If you're not here for a few months the story will disappear and you can start fresh again the next time. Otherwise, people will be asking about it and it could become a big negative."

I drove west from Hollywood along Sunset Boulevard, the only route I knew, towards my aunt and uncle's house in Pacific Palisades where I'd been staying. Instead of driving to the studio, I was driving away from it. Through gritted teeth and perhaps a damp eye, I vowed a terrific vengeance on all of Los Angeles. I would be back someday and they would all be sorry! I felt as much an outcast as Heathcliff in *Wuthering Heights* or Lopakhin in *The Cherry Orchard.*

I was encouraged to overcome this temporary setback by my mother who, with typical wisdom, sent me a column by Walter Winchell she had cut out of the newspaper. It was a "Who's Who" of show business, greats and near-greats recounting their numerous firings and disappointments. It seems that everybody who is anybody had been told to "get lost" at some time or another, some of them many times. I was never sure it wasn't going to happen again, especially since Actors' Equity Association permitted a producer to fire any actor before five days of rehearsal had passed without having to pay him any further compensation. It was always good to get past that fifth day.

Decades later I would have the great pleasure to work with Edward G. Robinson in an episode of Rod Serling's *The Twilight Zone* entitled "The Messiah of Mott Street." It was one of his last roles and I was delighted when he asked if I would come visit him in his trailer outside the sound stage and run lines with him before our scene was to be shot.

"I'm a little nervous on my first day," he said slightly out of breath from climbing the steps to the trailer, "I always am until I'm established. You know, until they come back the next day and say that the dailies were okay." The "dailies" were the scenes that were printed from yesterday's filming. The "powers that be" would watch them with a critical eye.

"Mr. Robinson," I said, "I can't believe that you could still be nervous after making eighty-seven films. Do you really think they would fire you?"

"Kid, they can do anything they want to in this business. So, don't ever get too comfortable." It took several years after my *Howie* fiasco for my confidence to return. I was always worried when the "suits" huddled in the corner of a rehearsal room or film set. Was this going to turn out like *Howie*? Have they discovered that I have no clothes on? Most actors I've known will confess fearing that they will be uncloaked, revealed, and exposed as charlatans.

I won an audition for the national touring company of Neil Simon's *Come Blow Your Horn.* The director was Stanley Prager, or "Stash," as he was known. He had stopped the show years earlier in a number from *The Pajama Game* called "Her Is." Stash was from the old school of comedy and practiced a consistent formula. The lights had to be bright, the furniture onstage had to be placed so that the actors could deliver the lines from as far downstage as possible, and all the "straight lines" had to be heard in the clear. He didn't want anybody "walking into" laughs. He demanded a crisp pace and clear articulation. He heard the play in his head as a series of good jokes interrupted by bits of important plot information.

One day he said to me, "Look, I know you're very idealistic and that your ambition is to become a "serious actor," but I'm going to ask you to do something really cheap. I don't expect you to like it, but if you do it, I promise you'll get the biggest laugh of the night."

I liked the idea of doing something cheap. It sounded like a chance to be part of a long tradition.

"What do you want me to do?" I asked Stash.

"I want you to get so angry with your father that when you say your line you jump in the air as high as you can on every single word of it."

"Really?" Now, I was dubious.

"I promise, it'll bring down the house."

He was right. It became my favorite moment of the play. Years later, when I was in *Victor/Victoria* with Julie Andrews, I complained to the director, Blake Edwards, that I didn't want to do a particular bit of business he had suggested because I felt it was too "cheap."

"I've made a fortune doing cheap," he said proudly. To his credit, he persuaded me to do it, and it worked.

I discovered early on that getting a laugh was like the feeling of a warm embrace on the side of my face. It could be that the mass exhalation of breath from a full house of people, all at the same moment, could be the cause of that warmth, but it's also an affirmation that you exist, and that others are affected by what you do. It's a high. It's like being super-alive. Al Pacino told me during the filming of *Serpico* that the reason he loved acting was because it gave him the chance to take a ride in the sky and not know where he was going to land. I'd add that it's also like walking a tightrope because it certainly matters to the audience, and to you, where you land. You had to be dangerous to be good, but not break your neck.

Al and I were both surprised by the success of *Serpico* and were hounded by people who wanted to know if we had smoked real pot during our scene. In the film, we were supposed to be in detective school and were given marijuana to sample, to understand its effects on a suspect's behavior. The fans were often disappointed that we didn't smoke real pot, but Al and I were too concerned about keeping pace with Sidney Lumet's shooting schedule to risk being "out of it," even though it may have looked that way on the screen.

It's funny how some actors prepare for their roles. I had a friend in college who wrote out his supposed inner thoughts, the ones that provoked his dialogue, called the "subtext," until his notebook weighed twice as much as his script. It was his bible during rehearsals, and after. I've known other actors who never made a note in the margin of their script, but knew exactly where they were in the context of their storytelling. In fact, Lumet once observed that he had never known an actor who couldn't convincingly start any scene in the middle, and not know where he was. To prove the point, *Serpico* was filmed backwards. Al's beard didn't appear until the second half of the picture, but he would never have had time to grow it if everything had been filmed in order.

Lumet liked to rehearse the whole movie as if it were a stage play before the actual shooting began. During one scene in the picture, I had a close-up as I listened to another actor seated close by. We shot the scene and after the first take, Sydney led me to a private area off the set.

"Everything you were thinking and feeling during that last take was perfect," he said. "Now, next time, I want you to do the exact same thing, only don't show it to me."

That was probably the best piece of direction I ever got. It was completely liberating because I could trust that the story would be told without my having to tell it. When it comes to acting, if you're doing it then you can't be watching it. Or if you're watching it, you can't be doing it. It's a trick. Otherwise Othello would strangle Desdemona and the show would close the next night There is real truth, and then there is aesthetic truth. As Spencer Tracy said to a greenhorn, "Take your hands out of your pockets, hit your mark, look the other actor in the eye, and tell the truth." Sounds simple, but it's harder than it looks.

I was twenty-three when I was cast in a prestigious, but unsuccessful, production of Saul Bellow's only Broadway play *The Last Analysis* starring Sam Levine. Sam had been in over forty Broadway plays, including the original production of *Guys and Dolls*, which I had seen three times when I was sixteen. He also had many good films to his credit. He had found a way to ground himself onstage in such a convincing reality that he was completely mesmerizing. For the first time in my stage career, I felt as if I was really being looked at and that he knew every thought in my head. I was playing his son. Unfortunately, as habit seemed to predict, on opening night he had forgotten to zip up his fly. During our scene together, it was my obligation to make him aware of it. He eventually caught on to my winks and glances and went upstage where, behind a large wing chair, he took the necessary steps to correct himself, so to speak. After my exit, the opening night crowd burst into spontaneous applause. I was never sure, and still am not, whether the applause was for my performance, or for getting Sam to close his fly. In either case, what did get closed was our play at the Belasco Theatre, after a two-week run.

Next up, I appeared in a play with Milton Berle at The Sahara Hotel in Las Vegas.

"What?!"

If he felt I hadn't said the set-up line loudly or clearly enough, he would yell "What?!" at me from across the stage. It was humiliating for me to have to repeat my line, but it only took two or three times to drive home the point. "When I get a laugh" he would say, "it's not *my* laugh, it's *our* laugh, and I can't get it without you." It was a great lesson in how to deliver a straight line. I never wanted to hear "What?" again.

Meanwhile I continued to audition hoping to get my big break. It came, as most breaks usually do, in a most unexpected way, by accident. Perhaps it was random fate, but it's still uncanny that baseball, the national pastime and a symbol of all that my father loved about America, should have been the setting for the most pivotal moment of my career.

I was sitting in the bleachers in Central Park watching a team made up of actors and stagehands from the Broadway production of *Barefoot in the Park*. They were playing their regularly scheduled Broadway Show League softball game. Robert Redford, the star, was about to take a vacation, and his understudy would be going on for him in the interim. Naturally, his understudy would need an understudy and I was hired to learn the part.

The understudy came up to bat and smacked the ball to the outfield for what looked like an easy single. As he rounded first, he saw a chance to stretch it into a double and headed full-speed for second base. He and the ball arrived at the same time and suddenly he was writhing in pain and holding his ankle. His teammates rushed to attend to him, but I just sat there. Could this be happening? Could this actor's bad break be *my* big break? And that's how it happened. I stepped into the role of Paul Bratter for the two weeks that Redford was gone. I was even asked to replace him permanently a few months later, after he left. I stayed in my first leading role on Broadway for eighteen months, playing opposite my college sweetheart, Penny Fuller. How lucky can a guy get?

One night after a performance, Woody Allen walked into my dressing room and introduced himself. I knew who he was, of course, and had recently auditioned for his first venture headed for Broadway, *Don't Drink the Water.*

"Hey," he stammered, after clearing his throat several times before he spoke. "You were …" (cough, cough) "…really good."

"Thanks," I said. "Thank you very much."

He cleared his throat some more and asked, "How come you do so poorly at the auditions?"

I had auditioned for David Merrick's production of his play no less than five times in the past few weeks.

"I guess I'm just lousy at auditions. I like to know the lines by heart before I can perform them." It was the only excuse I could think of.

"Ok…well…" (cough, cough) "…it's a good thing I came to see you in this play because, after five auditions…" (cough, cough) "…you weren't getting any better."

"Thanks a lot," I said. And I thought, "This could be the beginning of a beautiful friendship."

Woody Allen

The question I've been asked more than any other during my career has been, "Why do you and Woody Allen call each other Max all through *Annie Hall*."

It was Max's idea, rather, it was Woody's idea, the result of an incident that occurred as we were just getting to know each other. *Don't Drink the Water* was enjoying a modest run at the Helen Hayes Theatre. We were preparing for the upcoming Broadway Show League softball tournament and arranged to meet at the East 72nd Street and Fifth Avenue entrance of Central Park. I had my first baseman's glove under my arm and hurried up Madison Avenue on a bright, sunny afternoon in April. I didn't want to be late, and as I turned the corner I spotted him pacing agitatedly back and forth from about a block away.

"Woody!" I called out, wanting to announce my impending arrival. When I reached him he gently admonished me for speaking his name so loudly in a public space because it would attract attention, which he couldn't bear. I'll mention here that he was wearing sneakers, loose fitting khaki pants, a battle-worn (not by him) US Army field jacket, and an oversized floppy fisherman's hat.

"Don't you think it might be the outfit you're wearing that makes you such an eye-catcher?"

"Never mind that," he insisted. "Just please don't ever say my name out loud in public. I prefer to remain incognito."

"Oh," I paused. "Alright, I'll call you Max. No one will ever know it's you."

"Fine," he said, mollified.

And that was the last time the subject ever came up, although I did call him Max from that day forward whether in public or in the privacy of a backstage dressing room. This worked well for both of us until a few years later when I answered my phone and heard the familiar voice, but with a new greeting, "Hello, Max?" he said.

It took a moment to agree to this silliness, but I had the quick and appropriate comeback, "What is it, Max?" And that was it.

When I received the screenplay for *Annie Hall* I learned that he had included this double talk in our written dialogue and I never questioned the wisdom of it. It had the effect of making our friendship as authentic as any between two longtime pals. All relationships have particular quirks invented by one party or the other. Neither of us ever thought it would become an unanswerable trivia question, or one that I would be asked to answer during so many interviews.

Most of us find ways to avoid thinking about death, but Max is a philosopher by nature and skims through the works of Kierkegaard the way the rest of us read *People Magazine*.

"I don't understand how there can be *nothing*. It's not possible to conceive of such a thing. Even before there was God there had to be *something!* How can there be *nothing* without *something?*"

Meanwhile, my Chinese food was getting cold.

"Pass the duck sauce," I said. "Max, why don't you stop worrying about it? Stop torturing yourself. It can't be figured out."

While the rest of us have managed to push aside the big existential questions for most of our waking hours, he is doomed to ponder them, endlessly. Max uses the idea of man's finitude as a starting point from which to seize what life has to offer and make the most of it.

It's living itself that he respects, and his interests are as varied and numerous as any three people I have ever known. He knows the box scores of basketball games between teams that only a handful of sports fans could care about. He can tell you anything that was ever written in *Ring Magazine*, what the best films will be before they're shown at the New York Film Festival, and which galleries on Madison Avenue to stay away from. He also usually has the inside scoop on the latest scandal in Washington D.C.

Vacations are anathema to Max and thought of as cosmic waste. I once invited him, along with Diane Keaton, to spend a weekend at a small beach house I was hoping to purchase on Fire Island. It was a rare excursion for him to travel beyond Manhattan and he brought with him the largest piece of luggage I have ever seen. It was a giant black doctor's valise and also functioned as one. In it, there were enough antibiotics and antacids to open a small drugstore. He even brought a remedy for snake bite.

He made a begrudging visit to the beach, after spending the better part of the day reading the Times on the living room sofa, where he had spent the night. As long as I live I will never forget his Norman Maine inspired entrance into the Atlantic Ocean. He strode into the surf wearing his white skull cap for protection against scalp burn, then dove and flailed frantically as Keaton and I held our sides with laughter. It wasn't exactly James Mason in *A Star is Born*, but it was worth the price of admission. He tolerated the sun and the sand for a full day and a half before he fled by seaplane back to his Manhattan apartment.

Before he departed he left me a note on the kitchen table. I had left earlier in the day for the mainland in order to sign the closing papers for the house I wanted to buy. Anyone who has ever bought a house knows that there are endless forms to sign, loans to be taken out, taxes to be assumed, insurance to be transferred, and so on. The lawyer representing my interests in this transaction was a man named Arthur Silsdorf. For some reason, the name tickled Max, and he repeated it a few times himself. When I returned to the house after putting my John Hancock on a dozen or more documents, I glanced at the note Max had left for me. It said:

> "Max! This is urgent. Silsdorf is an impostor! He has arranged this entire closing as an excuse to steal your money. Don't sign anything!
>
> Love, Max."

As if that wasn't enough, almost a year later, I had the need to find a good analyst and asked Max to suggest someone. He had certainly researched the field. He gave me the name of a Dr. Herman Kliendeinst. I never actually contacted Dr. Kliendeinst because, the next day, I received a telegram from Max which said:

> "Max. Stop everything! Kliendeinst is really Silsdorf!"

Max overcame his natural shyness and tendency to be reclusive during the run of *Don't Drink the Water*. In the last act, there is a huge reception held at the US Embassy, where the play is set. There were nearly twenty people onstage at the same time holding champagne glasses and exchanging dialogue, which was mostly jokes and personal insults. Among the throng were two women in full Arab garb meant to be Sheik's wives from an unnamed middle eastern country. Why Max decided to portray one of the wives remains unknown but suddenly, to the cast's surprise, there he was among us. He wore a veil and slippers, so his presence went unnoticed by the audience. He had no lines, nor offered any. He did take a curtain call though, as I remember. It only happened once. Go figure.

He also asked his friend Mickey Rose, a comedy writer for *The Tonight Show* whom none of the cast or crew of *Don't Drink the Water* had ever met, to join us for the curtain call one night. He bowed with the rest of us from center stage wearing a novelty shop chicken mask and astonished the applauding spectators. I'm sure they compared notes after the curtain fell to figure out who the hell that was, and why he was there. There was no answer.

If you grow up in New York City then you know that you're either a Yankee fan or a Met fan. Max claims to be both, but I don't buy it. He taunts me about the Mets and roots for the Yanks when they face each other. He doesn't display much fervor, but loves the game. He also loves basketball but I've never known him to stand up in Madison Square Garden, even though he lives to follow the Knicks and is a season ticket holder. The entire arena will be on its feet but only a private expression of pleasure will cross his face. He once booked the Garden so he could film a scene that was intended to show him dribbling with Earl "The Pearl" Monroe. The scene never made it into the final cut, but he admitted to me later that the pure thrill of standing at center court with a basketball in his hand was as much joy as he could handle. As a matter of fact, he couldn't handle it. He couldn't bring himself to actually shoot the ball in the direction of the basket.

"It would have been too much," he told me.

"Too much what?" I asked.

"I don't know, just too wonderful."

Weird.

He happens to be a very good athlete, and we played together in the Broadway Show League when *Don't Drink the Water* and *Play it Again, Sam* had their runs. David Merrick's General Manager, Jack Schlissel, had given us money for uniforms, provided we name the team after him. We were known as Schlissel's Schleppers, and our jerseys said so. Woody played third base, Jimmy Burrows (the future director of *The Mary Tyler Moore Show*) played shortstop, the fine actor Murray Hamilton patrolled right field, and I pitched. *Don't Drink the Water* was one of the worst teams in the league, and usually lost by scores of 27-3 or

17-4. Yet every time we walked off the field Woody would assert that with a slightly better effort we could have won. He was as sure of this as he was that the sun would come up the next morning. I often tried to reason with him about it. "How could we win, Max? We have a lousy team. The other team was stocked with ringers from the stagehand's union and we're stuck with nine guys who put on make-up to make a living. We don't stand a chance!" But he remained optimistic and upbeat, until finally I told him to snap out of it.

Max wrote a line for me in *Annie Hall* in response to his question, "What are you doing out here in L.A., Max? You should be in New York doing Shakespeare in the Park!" The line for me was, "I already did Shakespeare in the Park, Max. Before I went on stage, two juvenile delinquents stole my tights." I had confided to him that I had a lot of trouble in Central Park. (In fact, I was robbed on the way to the subway as I was leaving the High School of Music and Art during my freshman year. Six guys surrounded my pal and me and demanded our money. It wasn't much but, to their credit, they made sure that we had enough left to pay our subway fare home. And they say New Yorkers are hard-hearted!)

I was in a scene in *Hannah and Her Sisters* in which a woman asks if I would donate my sperm to someone who wishes to become pregnant without having to bother about a significant other. In the script I'm a happily married man, but I'm flattered by the request nevertheless, and eager to comply. At that point, Max's character reminds me that I'm not being asked to have sex with anyone, just being asked to deliver the goods in a laboratory, and then disappear. The scene worked well, brief as it was, and provided a lighthearted moment in the middle of the film.

A few years later I was sitting in a restaurant, waiting for a friend, and the waiter slipped a note under my napkin. It was from two women at a nearby table who were inquiring if I could be so kind as to furnish them with some of my sperm. Of course, I made the connection to the scene from the movie, but have to confess I was disappointed to learn their invitation wasn't serious. It was just a joke. It's too bad. What a great story *that* could have been!

"Where'd you get that suit?" Max asked me, intoning the sound of Art Carney as Norton on *The Jackie Gleason Show* when he sits down at the counter and asks his pal Ralph Kramden, "What's that slop you're eat'in?"

He says this with an exaggerated tone of derision and proceeds to tell me that I'm dressed like a movie star. I'm being mocked. He prefers to blend in, or so he thinks, and disappear. He and Keaton would prowl around in lower Manhattan until they found some obscure remnant they saw as relevant to something long gone or else inventively new. I had just arrived in his apartment to read through the lines he had written for us in *Annie Hall*. We hadn't begun shooting yet.

"I swiped it from the wardrobe department of the last play I did. It's difficult to buy anything new considering the salary you pay."

This was not true. I was always appropriately paid, and we never discussed such matters. That stuff was handled by agents and producers. We were just wisecracking like two guys kibitzing in a locker room or during a game of chess.

We read our lines aloud, sitting across a table, and every once in a while he asked if I felt comfortable saying the lines as written, or if I would prefer to alter the structure of the line in some way. He would say, "Go ahead and say it any way you want, whatever's comfortable." This is a very nice way to work, I thought. He challenged me by saying that no matter what I said, when the picture was shown my line would still be the straight line, and his the punch line. And he was right, except on the occasion when I pulled a prank on him during the shooting of *Annie Hall*.

"We've got to go shopping," a wardrobe assistant said in the lobby of the Beverly Hills Hotel, where we were staying. "We'll go to Rodeo Drive and browse around. We need a jacket for your character to wear in the scene when you drive Woody home from jail."

In the Polo Shop, I spied the most ridiculous item I had ever laid eyes on. It was something you would never see on a real New Yorker unless he was a wacko. It was a white parka with a green plastic visor attached to its hood. There was even a way to button down the visor if you wanted to look like a race car driver.

"Can we get this?" I asked.

"Maybe for a laugh," she replied, "but we better bring along another option, just in case."

We got another option, but arranged to keep the heftily-priced white lab coat with hood and visor out of Max's sight until it came time to roll film and shoot the scene.

"Ready," said the assistant director.

Max yelled, "Action!"

We were in the front seat of a parked convertible and spoke our lines while I pretended to fumble with the ignition. When we came to the last line of written dialogue, I pulled the hood up on the top of my head and lowered the green plastic visor over my eyes. It was the first time anyone had seen it. To my surprise no one yelled "Cut!" and Max said, without missing a beat, "Max, are we driving through Plutonium?"

I never imagined he could think of something so quickly. But the assistant director didn't yell, "Cut!" and the camera was still rolling.

"It keeps out the Beta rays." I replied. "You don't get old!"

I'll never know where those words came from but they were there when I needed them and they stayed in the film. Max decided to do one more take just for protection. They always do a "safety take" because no one knows if the camera jiggled, or the focus was off, or the sound didn't record, etc. At the end of this second take, however, Max said, "Max, are we driving through a field of bees?"

I managed to keep a straight face and used the same closer. I couldn't get that lucky twice in a row. What began as a joke on Woody became one of the films best laugh lines.

"Why is something *great*?" Max asks, as we stroll through Central Park. "What is it that makes it *great*?"

"What are you talking about?" I say.

"Well, we know Beethoven was *great* right? And Picasso, and Shakespeare, but who decides that and what qualifies something to be known as *great*?"

"Maybe it's because its stood the test of time." I suggest. "Its been around long enough that it affects many generations of people all over the world."

He ponders this for a moment, but it doesn't satisfy his restless mind. He wants there to be a definitive reason why one piece of art is insignificant while another is deemed to be *great*. He wants it to apply to music, painting, writing, singing, films, theatre, etc. He's angry at the critics, and anyone else who presumes to know the answer to such a question. He objects to the brief but mostly damning reviews printed in the television listings when a movie is scheduled to be shown. They are the opinions of some unnamed employee at the paper who has been given the task of summing up the pluses and minuses of something once considered worth producing. Perhaps he is riled by a negative review of one of his own creations. This doesn't happen very much to Max, but if he can argue that it's impossible to define *greatness* then maybe it's also impossible to define *failure.* He's having trouble convincing himself. I'm pretty sure he doesn't believe that any of his own work qualifies as being *great*, despite being reminded almost daily that it is. He thinks Dwayne Wade is *great.* He is a point guard for the Miami Heat and Max wants him to move to New York and play for the Knicks. He's less interested in who sings *La Bohème* at The Met than who can challenge LeBron James under the basket. I'm out of answers, but offer my sympathy for his concern and frustration. What else can I do? What else could anybody do?

Max is thrilled if nobody knows he's in the room. He dons a baseball cap as soon as he steps out of his front door, and wears muted colors in an understated way. He once told me that the sweater he was wearing, which had cost a pretty penny, had been described by the salesman who sold it to him as the color "mustard" according to its designer. Woody said that under the lights at Madison Square Garden he thought it looked like dog shit. He doesn't go in for *fancy.*

All comics or comedians share the desire to render an audience helpless with laughter. (Milton Berle said, "A comic says funny things, but a comedian says things funny.") Thus the terms "I killed 'em," "I knocked 'em dead," "I layed 'em in the aisles," "I murdered 'em," and so on. Although Max is hardly ever *on* except when he's doing his act, by which I mean reaching out for a laugh, I recall a conversation we had during the out of town tryout of *Don't Drink the Water*. It was a big hit in 1966 and enjoyed a good run once it opened, but things out of town weren't going so well. David Merrick, the producer, wanted changes in the script and people were getting fired left and right. I had a leading role in it and had known Max for only a few weeks. We had hardly ever spoken. We were on a rehearsal break and lingering in the aisle at the rear of the empty theatre.

"What do you wish that your play would be that it isn't at the moment?" I asked.

"I want them to laugh as hard as they can until they beg for mercy! I want them to be unable to catch their breath. I want there to be no straight lines. I wish I didn't have to have them. I would like to go from one joke to the next without any pauses, unless they're necessary to hear the next line, of course."

He was very passionate about it, and becoming a little worked up. Needless to say, after that, we moved on to other subjects in a lighter vein. He was eccentric, but I had seen his routines as a comic and knew he was unique. It was impossible to know at the time the impact he would have on the world, or to predict the scope of his creative work, which has surpassed that of any film director in history.

So the three of us, Max, Keaton, and me, were sitting in a luncheonette in San Francisco, where we were filming *Play it Again, Sam.* Some people happened to wander over to our table and ask if I was a famous person. They eventually realized that I was sitting with Max and Keaton and, after a brief chat, they went on their way. Keaton pretended to be perturbed and asked why I was always the first one to be recognized instead of her or Woody. Max said, "It's because his head is too large and his hair is too big. He looks like a bowling ball. Anybody could see him. He stands out."

I had never outgrown my weight issues as a teenager, and I often shared these painful memories of inferiority with Max, especially when it came to ordering food. I wanted to fit into my wardrobe. Once in a while, he would teasingly refer to me as "Fatty," a sort of playful towel snap. That same night in San Francisco, our laughter attracted the attention of a small elderly lady at the next table, who could have been in the cast of *Arsenic and Old Lace*. She had just paid her check and must have been eavesdropping. On her way out, she leaned over my shoulder and said, in a commanding voice, "Well, have a nice meal, Fatty!" We gasped, and then roared. It reminded each of us how cruel and incidental the universe can be. Not to mention funny. We hurt from laughing.

During the filming of *Annie Hall*, it was discovered that my trailer had been broken into on Columbus Avenue, and all my belongings were missing, including the screenplay.

"They stole the script?" Max asked. He was aghast and became seriously concerned. He was thinking that perhaps Mel Brooks had taken it. I was more concerned that my wallet was gone, along with my checkbook, keys, and driver's license. A few days later the police reported that they hadn't been able to recover any of my belongings, but that the screenplay had been found in a garbage can, not far from where we had been shooting.

"I guess the thieves thought it was garbage, Max," I said.

A few months later, of course, it won the Academy Award for Best Picture of the Year.

The Max connection was a phenomenon that dwarfed my more modest accomplishments in ways that were beyond my comprehension. Nothing I had achieved in the theatre, in films, or on television prepared me for the recognition that came from being in six of Max's films. Nor did I ever expect that the relationship that evolved between us on screen would become as iconic as it has. Suddenly, or so it seemed, I had become Max, the character, which personified everybody's best friend and confidant. It was disorienting, in a way, because I was defined in a series of wildly successful films without having expected it. No one could have anticipated the impact they had on a generation of viewers all over the world. It has been decades since those films were first released and I have become accustomed to the familiar identification of myself as the fictional Max, but their impact was still a constant surprise as my career moved ahead. I benefited from this exposure to the extent that it was elevating, but it was also hard to shake off. Max and I apparently related onscreen in ways that were familiar to millions of guys who shared the same incongruities and intimacies with their own best friends.

"They like our schmoozing." he said to me after *Annie Hall* opened.

"Who does?" I replied.

"The audience. They want to see more of it."

That seemed just fine to me. It meant I would have another job, but was still startled to feel the affect of being that familiar to the hoards of strangers who, almost overnight, greeted me in the streets and everywhere else as if they'd known me all their lives. It reminded me of Milton and Mickey at the racetrack. A producer of the film remarked that I might have difficulty getting other work if this identity became too unshakeable. I often wondered if I had earned my fame at the expense of ever being cast as *Henry V*, or any other character with traits different from mine.

My agent submitted me for a role in an Oliver Stone film and I was treated with courtesy and respect, but told that I was too familiar an entity and that any audience, including Stone himself, would expect me to deliver a comedy performance, or at least a comic moment, in his otherwise dark view of Wall Street. He said his film just couldn't handle that. My agent was furious and claimed I was being typecast out of making a living, but there was no appeal to be made. On the other hand, I was suddenly a celebrity with all the accompanying perks, meaning good tables in restaurants, the best seats on airplanes, autograph seekers at openings, and offers of work, some worthy and others not.

Meanwhile, I couldn't help thinking that this was all a case of mistaken identity. The character of Max was the least challenging role I ever played. It grew comfortably out of the genuine chemistry between Max and myself and, of course, the truth and wit of his writing, but it never felt like climbing Mount Everest. I welcomed the acclaim, but also wondered if one day I might regret its cost. Fortunately, these films coincided with a string of five Broadway hits which would keep me employed by David Merrick for the next ten years of my life.

David Merrick

April, 1966

I was sitting at a front table in Sardi's restaurant waiting, in a state of disbelief, for the two men who had invited me there to have lunch with them. The two men were Harold Pinter and Robert Shaw. I knew that Pinter, who was later knighted by the Queen of England, was an important contemporary playwright, and Shaw had starred in some fine films. I was working up the street at the time in *Don't Drink the Water* and my agent had made the arrangements for this meeting. It seems that Pinter was set to direct the first production of a play by Shaw titled *The Man in the Glass Booth.* It was about the trial of Adolf Eichman, who had been tried in Israel a year earlier and was convicted of war crimes. The play was scheduled to open in London the following season starring Donald Pleasance and then transfer to Broadway. They had seen my performance and wanted me for the second lead in their project. This was too good to be true. I thought with this in my portfolio, I would have serious credentials. If I could manage not to be replaced along the way, I would go from being a light comic leading man to someone with authentic gravitas. Lunch went well and a few nights later Robert Shaw invited my agent, Milton Goldman, and me to his suite at the Plaza Hotel to hear his play.

After indulging in a few sips of wine, Shaw began to read aloud to us. Unfortunately, twenty minutes later he stopped reading. He had fallen asleep and his head was resting on his chest. We didn't want to alarm or embarrass him, so we tip toed out on our own. There was only one problem: I had to get David Merrick's permission to leave the play up the street in order for everything to work out.

A day later I showed up at Merrick's office with a carefully composed, handwritten letter asking him to replace me for the final three months of my contract. I reasoned that the audiences for it were starting to dwindle anyway and that my name, even though it was above the title, was not the drawing card. There would still be two bigger names than mine remaining: Lou Jacoby and Kay Medford. I told him in the letter that my greatest aspiration was to be a serious stage actor and that this was the opportunity of a lifetime; something any actor in America would be thrilled to accept. I would wait for his phone call.

When the call came the next day, his voice was gentle and his words, as always, were well thought out. These were his terms: if Harold Pinter would allow David Merrick to produce his next play in New York, then he would agree to let me out of my contract. At first, I was relieved because I didn't think that might be such a big deal. What I learned shortly after was that all of Pinter's plays on Broadway had been produced by Alexander Cohen, the President of The League of Broadway Producers, and Pinter had no wish to be disloyal to his brand, so to speak.

"That's blackmail!" said an outraged Pinter when I told him about Merrick's response to my letter. He went on to say some other strong things, but finally had to accept the idea that someone else would have to be found to play the part in his play. I was as disappointed as I'd ever been. To this day, I regret I wasn't able to take the job. The good news is that the part went to my closest friend from Northwestern, Lawrence Pressman, who did it in London and New York. I had nothing to do with it, but if it had to be somebody else, I was glad it was him. I also had to appreciate the fact that if Merrick hadn't insisted that Woody Allen come to see me in *Barefoot in the Park* and persuade him to cast me in *Don't Drink the Water* I would never have been noticed by Pinter and Shaw in the first place. I was angry with Merrick, who often referred to actors as children, and found it difficult to forgive him for depriving me of that next rung on the ladder. He wanted to insure that I would be available to play the lead in his next Broadway blockbuster *How Now, Dow Jones*. It wasn't a blockbuster like *Hello, Dolly*, but it ran for a season and I was nominated for a Tony Award for Best Actor in a Musical. I've often wondered how I would have felt if the creators of that show had not been in agreement with him when it came to casting me in the lead. Maybe they had no choice, but he still took a big gamble with my future when he kept me from going abroad.

Despite Merrick's vote of confidence in me, I still had to audition for the creative team. Fortunately, I had studied with David Craig, who taught many actors how to apply their acting skills to fit the demands of performing "in song." During a song, you can't just say the lyrics when you feel like it. You have to follow the discipline of a time signature. There is a conductor and other musicians, and obviously everybody has to play together. David Craig taught a technique that some actors grasped after only a few weeks while others struggled for months, but once they understood it, they could rely on it for the rest of their lives. Some of his best students could barely produce a sustained note, but their thoughts and feelings were expressed in a way that fit the demands of a composer and a conductor. For the real nitty gritty of it you'll have to read one of his books (it's well worth it), but here is his shortened audition procedure:

1. Start from nothing. Be a blank canvas.
2. Find the light.
3. Sing to a spot.
4. Nod to the accompanist.
5. Play the pauses.
6. Play the ride out.
7. Get back to zero.

As soon as I sang the last note of my audition for *How Now, Dow Jones*, Merrick joined me onstage, along with my agent, and immediately made his offer of salary and the length of the contract. It was an awkward moment for me and my representative, but there was no way to bargain under those circumstances. Merrick got what he wanted.

I never discussed my feelings with Merrick. He was always courteous, soft spoken in a lawyerly fashion, but he brought a sense of power into a room when he entered it; an unspoken threat that you better not give him any trouble. He used to hang his overcoat in my dressing room when he came to see a run-through or performance. Often, he took a seat and chatted about his troubles with other shows in progress out of town. I was a sounding board for his thoughts, but I was much too awed to make any suggestions. I was harmless and always polite. He obviously liked my work. He hired me five times. He also liked me because he could hear me. I was loud onstage and once pleaded with him not to mic me up, which is the norm in musicals today, but wasn't in 1967. Merrick was a little hard of hearing, but I finally persuaded him to let me use my own volume controls instead of giving over that authority to a sound technician in the rear of the house. *How Now, Dow Jones* was one of the last shows to be done without mic-ed actors.

Even with the success of those five shows, I was still living a double life. In my mind I was just a comer. My big breaks were always in front of me, up ahead. I was still a spear carrier in the chorus, despite my very tangible success. At the age of thirty I was sitting on top of the world in ways few of my colleagues could boast of. But, like most other actors I've known, I was afraid of being unmasked. They would find out that I didn't know what I was doing and I would be exposed as a fraud. I had gotten lucky, that's all. Luck, it's been said, is the residue of design. Maybe, or maybe not.

Don't Drink the Water was a hit with audiences. The critics thought it was a mixed bag. It was outrageously funny and bordered on theatre of the absurd. Merrick once remarked that he wouldn't rest until his productions filled every legitimate theatre on Broadway. At one time he had five shows running at the same time. Even then, there was a sign in his office which read, "It is not enough for us to succeed. Our competitors must fail!"

Woody was braver than I was because he grew up in Brooklyn, whereas I was a softy from Manhattan. David Merrick, the most notorious powerhouse on Broadway, was giving him some harsh criticism about the plot of *Play it Again, Sam* and Woody said to him in a very calm voice, "Listen, David, I've made a lot of money in my life by not listening to men in blue suits." which, of course, Merrick was wearing at the time. That was as hot as it ever got between them, but clearly, Woody was not going to be pushed around.

Merrick was notoriously critical when something onstage displeased him. He wasn't blunt to be cruel, but it got the best results. He terrified people from all walks of life, not because he hollered at them, but because of his unvarnished honesty, mostly delivered in a subdued, but purposeful tone. He sent out Christmas cards with a sketch of Santa Clause hanging from a noose, to reinforce his reputation as a curmudgeon. His efforts earned him the moniker, '"The Abominable Showman."

He was at the top of his field and had a fierce determination to turn out hits. He treated me well, but I never felt that I got to know him on a personal level. When Merrick, as everybody called him, visited the theatre, he was usually in the company of his business partners. They all wore the same black overcoats, white scarves, and large fedoras.

Sitting in my dressing room, he confided to me that he didn't enjoy playing the role of marriage counselor, but that the process of producing a good musical required him to do so. "My job is to get the lyricist to write a song that fits the scene that led up to it, instead of what the lyricist preferred to write. It's the same with all the others. If they aren't forced to cooperate, they'll each write what they want and the show will be lousy."

In order to accomplish this, he threatened to replace people and kept a shadow team of creators ready to jump into the mix on short notice. I saw him fire some dancers in the wings in the middle of a performance because he couldn't persuade the choreographer to make do with a smaller ensemble.

How Now, Dow Jones was written by Elmer Bernstein, Carolyn Leigh, and Max Schulman. The idea for it came from a conversation on a plane to Los Angeles between Lee and Bernstein, who had never met, but found themselves seated together on the flight. The story was that some low-level attractive female employee of a big stock market firm would falsely announce that the Dow Jones Industrial Average had finally risen above one thousand points. She would do this because it was part of a scheme to get her boyfriend to marry her. That was the plot for the first act when we began rehearsals. They hadn't figured out the second act yet, but that was of no great concern since all shows went out of town in those days to get "whipped into shape." There would be plenty of time to worry about the second act later.

"Later" turned out to be the third week of rehearsals in New York before the out-of-town tryout. We still didn't have a plot. The creators were watching us work our way through a particularly confusing scene in the middle of the second act. They each had a different idea of how the scene should end. There were a lot of suggestions, but nothing was resolved. Finally, with some trepidation, I asked plaintively if someone could simply tell me the plot of the second act.

"How does the story end?" I implored them to tell me. "If I don't know what the plot is, then I can't bring any sense to any of the lines you've given me to say."

It may have been uppity of me, but it moved the process forward, at least until we opened in Philadelphia where an entire new version of the second act was presented to the cast. It was the first of several experiments to solve the problems of the show. We were truly characters in search of an author.

Our first director was Arthur Penn, who had recently finished making the iconic film *Bonnie and Clyde*. On the first day of rehearsal he confided to me that he had never directed a musical before, but hoped this would be a helpful learning experience. We opened out of town to dreary notices and poor Arthur was dismissed, to the dismay of the cast who all loved him.

Fortunately, Merrick brought in the famous George Abbott to save the day, and he did. He had just turned eighty, but had the energy of a lion. He was more like a field marshal than anything else. Also replaced out-of-town was Gillian Lynne, who would choreograph *Cats* a few years later. Her replacement was Michael Bennett, the genius behind the yet-to-be-conceived *A Chorus Line.*

Mr. Abbott took charge and advised me not to play the jokes. "The laughs will come if you play the character. Your job is to be interesting. Let the playwright take care of what's funny." It wasn't uncommon for him to send the writers back to work on dialogue that he deemed substandard. "I can't ask the actors to learn this. It isn't fair."

How rare it was to hear that from a director, and how we all appreciated it. *How Now, Dow Jones* ran for six months at the Lunt-Fontanne Theatre and I was nominated for the Tony Award for Best Actor in a Musical. It closed as a result of a strike called by Actors' Equity Association just as ticket sales were starting to wane. I was serving a term as an elected member of the Actors' Equity Association Board of Directors and found it peculiar to be waving a strike sign under my own marquee. Merrick refused to reopen it after the strike. I was twenty-eight years old and decided to indulge in one of my enduring fantasies, a six-week tour of the Far East.

I went to Southeast Asia, inspired by Joseph Conrad whose works I had been assigned to read in high school. I used my bonus money from an industrial I had just finished to pay for my pilgrimage to the exotic, faraway places described in his tales of adventure.

An industrial is a theatrical production meant to sell a product line to a sales force. (Funny how manufacturer's deliver a product to a sales force, theatre delivers entertainment to an audience, and network TV delivers an audience to a sponsor.) They can be very elaborate, and this was the daddy of them all known as *The Milliken Show*. It ran for almost three weeks each spring. The show would start at eight in the morning and last about an hour. The Milliken Company, based in North Carolina, would fly in hundreds of out-of-town buyers from department stores all over the country. They were registered in hotels and bussed to and from the Waldorf-Astoria Hotel, where the show was performed in the Grand Ballroom. There, they served an excellent breakfast and were entertained by top-line stars and dancers from current Broadway shows, who paraded before them in the new styles and fabrics being hawked by the Millikens. It was tough for everyone to sparkle at that hour, especially if you were working on a Broadway schedule, but it was worth it. The pay was high and, after the final performance, the entire company sat on the floor in a circle as each of us was given an envelope full of cash. At the time, the average bonus was two thousand dollars, enough to do something special. I used it to fund my trip to the Far East.

Of course, I didn't know a soul in Singapore, so when the phone rang in my hotel room at 4:00am, I thought it had to be a mistake. "Hello, Tony. Are you having a good time?" It could only be a dream, a nightmare, or David Merrick. "How long are you going to hang around Asia? I may need you to get on a plane very quickly."

His new musical *Promises, Promises* was opening that night in Boston on its way to Broadway and, in typical fashion, Merrick was looking for backup in the event that the critics found cause to complain. As it turned out, Jerry Orbach opened to rave reviews and went on to win the Tony Award for his performance. The show was a huge success. It had a book by Neil Simon and music by Burt Bacharach and lyrics by Hal David. A year later, I was asked to star in the London production and leapt at the chance. What a unique opportunity it was for an American actor to appear, let alone star, in a West End theatre. It was especially gratifying because I still regretted that I hadn't made it to London in *The Man in the Glass Booth*. I was just short of my thirtieth birthday and my luck was riding high.

Before *Promises, Promises* kicked into gear, I had spent ten months playing Dick Christy opposite Diane Keaton and Max himself in *Play it Again, Sam*. It was the experience that greased the wheels of our friendship. Max was more accustomed to doing stand-up than having to recreate credible interaction with other characters night after night. During one performance, he glanced at the front row and saw two nuns sitting there. For some reason, this brought him to such uncontrollable spasms of laughter that he had to leave the stage. Keaton and I ad-libbed until he returned, which wasn't long but it was unnerving. (Max was in the habit of pacing in my dressing room before each performance, and again at intermission, before his Orange Julius arrived. He refused to go on without one. At some point, Keaton and I, who loved him to bits, had to tell him that he was totally out of his mind. He already knew that, so telling him didn't make a difference.)

British Equity, the actor's union in England, allowed only five Americans to be in the cast of *Promises, Promises*, including Betty Buckley and myself, and we were grateful for the opportunity. One day, when we finished rehearsals at The Prince of Whales Theatre, I was invited by Merrick and his London co-producer, Binky Beaumont, to attend the opening night performance of another of their offerings, the London version of *Play it Again, Sam*, which I had just left in New York. It starred Dudley Moore, and I was eager to see it.

I sat in the second row of the balcony, just behind the two producers. The curtain rose to reveal the lead character, Alan Felix, alone in his apartment watching a Bogart movie on TV and popping aspirins. I looked down at the set and something about it seemed amiss. Maybe it was the slightly different furniture or the scale of the set to the size of the theatre, but something wasn't right. And then, suddenly, I realized what it was. The phone was missing. The prop department had forgotten to place a phone on the desk downstage right. If ever a prop was as important as this one, I'd never heard of it.

The character of Dick Christy spends the first ten minutes on the telephone, and the actor playing the role was about to make his entrance and go straight for it. This was before the advent of cell phones and Christy is obsessed with keeping in touch with his office. He leaves his number wherever he goes so he is never out of touch. I alone, in all the world, knew what was coming. I leaned forward and whispered into the producer's ears, "There's no phone."

This information didn't elicit much of a reaction from them. After all, they weren't the poor souls onstage who would have to find a way to solve this. There is nothing worse on an opening night than to discover that a prop is missing. I watched in horror as my counterpart onstage discovered the problem. He couldn't very well pretend that he was holding a phone when there wasn't one and as the other actors onstage realized what had happened each took it upon themselves to solve the problem.

Dudley Moore said, "I think I've got another phone in the bedroom!" and he exited through a door stage right. The actor playing my role did not wish to be stuck onstage until his return and, after a feeble ad-lib to his wife, chimed in, "No, no, I think there's a phone in the kitchen." and exited stage left. The remaining actress decided to look for her own phone and disappeared through a slot in the set not yet made use of, but which permitted an exit during a dream sequence later on. The audience had no idea where she went or how. They only knew that the stage was now empty, but not for long. All three returned shortly from different directions, two of them carrying telephones. After a while, the play found its footing and continued quite nicely.

No such problems befell *Promises, Promises* on its opening night. It went perfectly. Two days earlier, Neil Simon, who wrote it, insisted on taking me out to lunch. I knew there was something important he wanted to tell me and it was memorable.

"You know, when I write a play, I construct it as if it were a sporting event. The protagonist is like the home team. The audience wants him to win or achieve his heart's desire, whatever it may be. Then I invent all sorts of obstacles to put in his way, which creates conflict and tension. In the end, the protagonist gets what he wants and the audience goes home happy. A good comedy is not too complicated when broken down like that, but in order for it to work, the protagonist must want what he wants so badly that the audience is rooting for him to get it every moment of the play. You, the actor, have to communicate that 'want' to the audience. The more you love the girl, the more the audience wants you to win her. You're the hero, the home team!"

I got the message. Donna McKechnie stopped the show cold during the first act, and the company took no less than twenty curtain calls to a standing crowd during the final bows. I was awakened the next morning by the press agent for the show who called to read me the notice from The London Times. The reviewer was Harold Hobson:

> "All London should crowd to see Anthony Roberts in *Promises, Promises* (Prince of Whales). What is more, all London will, for this Burt Bacharach musical is a wild success. Mr. Roberts is witty; emphasizes his diffidence with exactly the degree of confidence that is paradoxically necessary; sings and dances well; and moves with beautiful precision. But the unique quality of his performance is a chivalry that derives from a deeply realized generosity and human feeling. The world is a finer as well as a more enjoyable place because of the nature of Mr. Roberts' performance. Go and see him. If you live to be a hundred you won't regret it."

"My God," I thought. "I couldn't have written a better review myself."

I went on to win the London Critic's Poll Award, the British equivalent of a Tony

Award at the time, and received—on royal stationary—an invitation to High Tea at Buckingham Palace. Naturally, I shared this news with my pals at the theatre, including my dresser and personal valet for the show, Mr. David Denyer.

David Denyer was nothing if not precise. He worked as a dresser in London, and often for Sir Alec Guinness. David was most fulfilled when standing at attention in the wings, out of dutiful respect, waiting for the exact moment to hand an actor his hat, or cane, and when to pour his tea (or other liquids) after the show. He was appalled by my robe, and insisted on keeping a silk one on hand because, according to him, I would be visited frequently by royals and other important dignitaries. He was of medium height, about fifty, slightly bald, and rail-thin. He was like something out of Dickens, a century behind the times and proud of it.

His role in life was to be there, literally behind the scenes, but at the same time, not be there. He was witness to many privacies when helping testy and perspiring actors in and out of their costumes. By merely being present, as a matter of need, he heard conversations that were, at times, inappropriately intimate, emotional, and stormy, but David was the ultimate professional and determined to be perfectly servile at all times while still staying one step ahead of the game. His sense of humor, elegant dignity, and great respect for Americans made it a pleasure to see him for six months of eight performances a week.

When I shared my invitation to Buckingham Palace with Mr. Denyer, he was not convinced that it was authentic and, after further investigation, it did, indeed, prove to be a forgery. A disgruntled ex-employee of the palace staff was sending the same invitation to several persons in London who had received recent notoriety. Some unsuspecting victims had even gone to Buckingham Palace expecting to enjoy tea and crumpets with the Royal Family.

I was suddenly involved in a fabulous hoax that headlined the London tabloids for almost three weeks. There was something about it in the papers every day. At one point, two aggressive reporters accosted me backstage as I was about to make an entrance, assuring me that their questions wouldn't take long to answer. This led to some mild shoving and, eventually, they were led out of the theatre by the stage manager, the doorman, and the frail but fastidious and iron-willed Mr. Denyer.

During the run, I was asked to appear in a charity review to celebrate the occasion of Sir Noël Coward's 70th birthday. It was held in a packed theatre and began at midnight so that all the stars currently playing in the West End could participate. I performed a song from an early Coward review with Nicky Hanson, a popular figure in the English theatre scene, and Bryan Forbes, the film director.

Climbing the steep staircase up to the stage from the cavernous basement was slow-going because so many performers were on their way down. I was agog. There was Susannah York in front of me, Dame Edith Evans behind me, and Sir Robert Morley leaning on the banister. I felt like an imposter, but I was treated by all with great kindness and respect.

My number went off without incident and, at three o'clock in the morning, the entire cast of fifty sat in chairs onstage before a full house and sang *Happy Birthday* to Noël Coward. It had been a memorable night, but his "thank you" speech was particularly eloquent and included a suggestion well worth remembering. He said, "Dear friends, and fellow artistes, where in the entire universe could anybody find a cast like this and an audience like this? I am deeply moved, but I had an acting teacher once who cautioned me, "Don't ever lose yourself on a stage, for, if you do, you will lose your audience as well." I certainly wouldn't want to lose this audience. So… all I can say is thank you, and goodnight."

Promises, Promises stirred up so much publicity that EMI, the largest record-producing company in England, asked me to record a single for the pop charts. The song they wanted me to sing was *Raindrops Keep Falling on My Head* by Burt Bacharach. It had already been released in the United States sung by B.J. Thomas and was a hit on the airwaves. We recorded it in the same studio where The Beatles had made *Abbey Road.* There were elaborate lighting fixtures overhead used to create various atmospheres at any hour of the day or night and, although The Beatles weren't anywhere to be seen, I was introduced to the engineer under exclusive contract with them, who was becoming something of a celebrity himself.

I never thought that *Raindrops* from the soundtrack of *Butch Cassidy and the Sundance Kid* was the best song for me. It had a drawling, cowboy lilt to it, and the nearest I usually came to a horse was in a movie theatre. Obviously, a great number of people agreed with me because, despite a six-week grace period before the B.J. Thomas version was introduced in England, very few of my records were purchased. My father bought three copies, and others in my family chipped in as well, but the Thomas version became as big a hit in England as it was in America, and deservedly so.

There would be one more show to do for David Merrick and that would be *Sugar*, based on Billy Wilder's film *Some Like it Hot.* The director was Gower Champion and the music and lyrics were by Jule Styne and Bob Merrill with a book by Peter Stone. Michael Crawford, the original star of *The Phantom of the Opera*, once told me, "In England, they wouldn't think of asking an actor to audition if he had any track record at all." Such is not the case on this side of the Atlantic. Even after starring in several successful Broadway shows, I still had to audition for *Sugar* because Jule Styne, who had written the score, had never heard me sing. As luck would have it, I was at a party the week before my scheduled interview. Jule came over, introduced himself, and said if I agreed to sing for him right then and there, he wouldn't ask me to come in and audition for him at the theatre.

He led me to a grand piano in a large living room filled with partygoers, more of his generation than mine, and quieted everyone down. Among the guests were Burton Lane, who happened to have written the song I was prepared to sing. He was persuaded by Jule to accompany me as I sang *Every Night at Seven*, first sung by Fred Astaire in *Royal Wedding*. After the song there was a round of applause from the guests at the party. Jule handed me a drink, put his hand on my shoulder, and told me I had the job. Whew!

Robert Morse and I had to be dressed as women for most of the show and the heels were killers. Great care was taken at the photo session to ensure that Bobby and I looked convincingly feminine. Make-up artists hovered over us for hours with devices to lift our brows, while earrings were clamped on us, and wigmakers glued flaps of netted hair over our sideburns. These pictures would appear on posters in Shubert Alley and on the sides of buses. We even made the cover of *Gay Scene* magazine. I could hardly recognize myself.

"I look just like my mother!" I exclaimed. I'd never wanted to become my mother that I know of, but she was an attractive woman and I could have done worse. I had a difficult time deciding which I hated more, the earrings or the high heels.

All in all, I had a very good relationship with David Merrick. Only once did he find it necessary to reprimand me, and even that was done with a wink of his eye. I was late making an entrance during a performance of *Play it Again, Sam* that he happened to attend. Missing an entrance is tantamount to committing murder. The life being simulated onstage is suddenly suspended and the actors onstage must improvise something so that the audience doesn't completely drop out of their involvement in the play. It happens very rarely. I knew he would show up in my dressing room after the show and went to great pains to beat him to the punch. I borrowed a length of rope from the prop table after the final bows and attached one end to the ceiling fan in my dressing room. I tied the rest of it around my neck and stood on a chair directly beneath it.

"Come in, please, Mr. Merrick." I called in response to his knock on the door, and he did.

He instantly grasped the situation and turned slyly to one of his assistants.

"Kick away the chair." He intoned with deadly seriousness. After a brief pause, we all had a good laugh. Needless to say, it never happened again.

When my Merrick period ended, I began to make more trips to Los Angeles in search of television work, as most of the shows were made there. Making a pilot is a real crap shoot. Walter Matthau appeared in the pilot for *The Guide for the Married Man,* in which I recreated the role he had played in the film. After shooting his scene, he said, "Well, Tony, I hope it sells or doesn't sell, whatever you wish." and then he winked at me, "You know, sometimes it's better if they don't sell."

During the run of *Promises, Promises* in London, I was blessed to meet and fall in love with Jennifer Lyons, a dancer in the cast and eventually the mother of my daughter, Nicole. We were wed at Marble Arch Synagogue and celebrated by a large and supportive cast full of friends and well-wishers. The marriage itself only survived a few years, but we remained friends despite the anguish that accompanies any divorce and are proud that our love produced our wonderful daughter, who has brought us both such joy.

Phase Three:
Get Me Tony Roberts!!

As I began to be recognized, I made a pact with myself: I was determined not to expect it, and never to be disappointed if it didn't occur. I reasoned that those who live by the sword will die by the sword and that fame wasn't going to destroy me. It first started happening when I had a recurring role on the daytime soap opera *The Edge of Night*. I was twenty-four at the time and suddenly found myself surrounded by a lot of women in Macy's looking for bargains in the basement. They tended to be soap opera fans and they would say, "Aren't you Lee Pollack from that TV show?" Other women would hear this and look over, and a moment later, I was like a piece of merchandise on the table. I was public property. It was flattering to be identified, but I was struck by how awkward it felt to be addressed as if I were Lee Pollack and not Tony Roberts. I wanted to tell them—and often did—that I wasn't really Lee Pollack. I was just an actor hired to play that role. I wanted to tell them that my real aspirations were much more ambitious and noble, and that I would strive to produce more "worthy" art as I moved forward in my career. (Talk about being full of one's self!) I was kidding myself to think they would want to hear a word of that. I was Lee Pollack, and they had discovered me in Macy's basement.

A few years later Senator Joseph Biden, a favorite of mine during C-SPAN debates, extended his hand to me as I strolled past the Regency Hotel on Manhattan's Upper East Side. His face lit up when he recognized me, and he said he wanted to thank me for all the pleasure I'd given him through the years. That's a nice way to start the day.

Johnny Depp stopped dead in his tracks as I was leaving a restaurant in Midtown and said with amazement, "You're a hero to me, man. You're Tony Roberts!"

"Aren't you supposed to be in jail?" I asked, because his face had been on the front page of the previous day's New York Post, and everyone in town knew that he and his girlfriend had been arrested after a fracas in their hotel room that had brought the police to the scene.

"Yes," he said. "I'm Johnny Depp. Marlon Brando got me sprung from a holding cell in New Jersey, where the cops wouldn't believe I wasn't an imposter. Marlon spoke to them over the phone and convinced them to let me go. It's an honor to meet you, Mr. Roberts."

John Lennon approached me at a counter in Bloomingdale's and shook my hand. "I just wanted to tell you how much I appreciate your work!" I looked back over my shoulder to see if he was speaking to me, or somebody else. I was dumbfounded.

I was sitting alone at a table in J.G. Mellon's on Third Avenue and suddenly, between my mouth and a hamburger, a huge black hand entered the picture. I glanced up at the largest set of perfect white teeth I have ever seen. It's Patrick Ewing of the New York Knicks, who is a fan and wants to introduce himself. How did this happen? When did I become so familiar to people I'd never met? Recognition is a welcome reward but hard to figure, especially when it comes from those who are so easily recognizable themselves.

I suspect that most of it had to do with being in a string of Woody Allen movies in the 1970s and 1980s. Unwittingly, I had become the tolerant, loyal, understanding, but often-frustrated friend of everyone's favorite eccentric. I didn't write that character into the script, but it wasn't far from the truth.

At Phase Three (Get me Tony Roberts!!), most actors are enjoying the "ink," or publicity, coming their way. Exposure pays off and it's worth investing some of your income by hiring a press agent when there is something worth blowing your horn about. A press agent of one's own, or one hired by the studio or producers, is paid to see that your name and face are seen in strategically prominent places. This isn't easy to do, because there are so many others competing to get themselves noticed as well. Many headshots and anecdotes wind up in lesser venues like the tabloids where one's image is not under any purposeful control. Many unintended consequences are the result. There are too many stars fighting for a limited number of quality interviews and media space. The old school of thought was that all publicity was beneficial, whether favorable or not, just as long as they spelled your name right. Fame can be a double-edged sword. I once sat in a car next to Milton Berle on our way from Phoenix to Las Vegas, where we would appear together in a production of *Never Too Late*. Before we got out of the car to grab some lunch at a Howard Johnson's restaurant, he buttoned his coat to the top of his neck, put on a dark pair of sunglasses, and pulled his hat down over his forehead. "Now," he said, "if nobody recognizes me, I'll kill myself." But in the long run it *does* matter how you're perceived by the public, as well as by those in the business. It's not good if your reputation as a responsible professional is compromised. It's also worth noting that nobody can possibly read everything that's written about them, and celebrities may not be aware of the latest rumors circling around them until it's too late to do anything about it. Some fans relate to me as Julie's "love interest" because I appeared on *The Love Boat* while others see me as a corrupt boxing promotor, which I played on *Law & Order*. Am I the sympathetic friend of Max, or the detective who smokes marijuana on a subway platform with Al Pacino in *Serpico*? I'm none of the above, and all of the above.

At *my* Phase Three, I was trying to choose the best projects available to advance my career and the options were varied. More often than not, they were merely a chance to tread water. Treading water isn't so bad because it provides income, with which you can hire a press agent. Press agents have to be paid by somebody and, unless you are the headliner on a project, the producer will want only the big box office stars publicized, but that doesn't mean you can't blow your own horn any way you can. I payed a press agent to keep my name in front of people in the business as much as possible. It was an investment I hoped would pay off later. They didn't teach this stuff at Northwestern, but I was learning it first hand. Treading water beats drowning any day.

I'm reminded of a bit of wisdom attributed to Burgess Meredith, an old pro of stage and screen familiar to many as George in *Of Mice and Men*. He was referring to the ability of any actor's agent to affect the ups and downs of his clients' career. Meredith said, "If the actor is hot, then the agent has an easy time of it. All he really has to do is answer the phone, but if the actor's not, there's not really much he can do to warm him up."

At Phase Three, it's all about the paycheck versus the artistic merit. My agent explained to me that the longer I didn't appear in any network programming, the fewer opportunities I would be offered and my salary would be noticeably diminished. So, it makes sense to "make hay while the sun shines," but this approach often leads you to compromise your own taste. Many of the opportunities that came in Phase Three fell into this category and were what even the titans of the industry refer to as just run-of-the-mill "product."

On the other hand, I was proud to work for the Circle Repertory Company in New York, founded by a classmate of mine from Northwestern, Marshall Mason. I was in

Lanford Wilson's *Serenading Louie*, Edward Albee's *Who's Afraid of Virginia Wolf?*, and a production of Chekhov's *The Seagull.* They were all done "out-of-town," meaning at the lowest salary permitted by Actors' Equity, but they were good for the soul. They were challenging and noble enterprises because they were done for love instead of money.

On the other side of the track was the swank life provided by the Beverly Hills Hotel which, luckily, had a business deal with the William Morris Agency around the corner, so their clients always got a good rate on a room. I wanted to create the impression that there were a lot of things happening for me all the time. And there were.

> "Tony Roberts was a triple-threat busy guy on Academy Award night. You could have seen him any place around the world—behind a Polaroid camera on the Academy Award show, with Woody Allen and Diane Keaton in *Annie Hall*, and as Petruchio in *The Taming of the Shrew* at the Alliance Theatre in Atlanta,

> GA. No waiting on the unemployment line for this actor!
>
> -The Hollywood Reporter, April 10, 1978

The truth was that I rarely knew I had a "next gig" until the gig I had was over.

Of course, there were the inevitable flops. *Murder at the Howard Johnson's* was a comedy about marital infidelity. The biggest laugh came at the beginning of the third act when the curtain rose to reveal the three leading characters on their knees hammering nails into a makeshift crucifix on which they planned to execute an unsuspecting interloper. It didn't run long, at least not on Broadway, although it was resurrected and enjoyed an extended life on the road and in international productions.

January, 1972

Not everyone gets to play Hamlet in front of the New York critics, and I never did, but I did play it when I was thirty-six years old with a cast of college students, including an eighteen year-old senior who played Gertrude.

The fact that this was taking place in Westerville, Ohio didn't make it press-worthy, but I considered it a major accomplishment. I read every book I could find about Hamlet and concluded that most of them contradicted each other in so many ways that it was impossible to resolve all the questions posed by so many interpretations. The bard himself surely couldn't have imagined all the various subtexts of this play unless he had lived many times as long.

On the eve of our first performance, I addressed the director in my dressing room.

"Are these kids out front going to believe that I'm Hamlet? I mean, I'm thirty-six years old and the rest of the cast is half my age."

He cut to the heart of the matter: "The way I see it, since you are the only one who knows the lines and the only one who showed up to say them, I don't think they have any choice."

I was calmed by his answer. After all, I had the tights, the sword, and the lines. I was the only Hamlet in the building.

My greatest challenge playing Hamlet was not to look down while speaking from the shallow, student-built precipice that represented the high parapet where my first scene took place. I didn't need to do any striding around, but my knees couldn't be shaking either. The ghost of my father hadn't even appeared yet!

We gave sixteen performances in all, and some of them began at nine o'clock in the morning before an audience of inner-city high school students from Columbus, Ohio. They took a while to settle down and, at times, shot rubber bands at us, but Shakespeare knew what he was doing, and soon enough we could hear a pin drop in all the right places. The villains were appropriately hissed and we could hear the kids rooting for Hamlet to solve his dilemma. Playing the part itself is like trying to inhabit a shadow. Any actor will bring some particular truth to it, which only his sensibility could, regardless of age or level of expertise.

I was in a summer stock production of *Serenading Louie* when my agent called with an offer to co-star in a play by Alan Ayckbourn called *Absurd Person Singular* starring Geraldine Page, Sandy Dennis, Richard Kiley, Carole Shelley, and Larry Blyden. I would have been thrilled to be in a play with any of these people, but to be in a play with all of them was a high point of my career. We were a hit and ran for more than a year at The Music Box Theatre, considered the crowning jewel of Broadway houses.

During the course of the run, as is often the case, we were visited backstage by politicians and celebrities. Handshakes and pleasantries were exchanged while cameras flashed and press agents beamed. The character I portrayed onstage was a particularly insensitive and callow fellow. His infidelities had caused his wife to attempt suicide. When Golda Meir, the Prime Minister of Israel, arrived after the final curtain, the cast formed a reception line to greet her. We were still in our costumes. When she got to me, she pressed my hand with both of hers, leaned forward, and with an entre-nous wink in her eye said, "Tsk, tsk, you're a very naughty boy." I giggled nervously, the same way I had when my grandmother chastised me for peeking at her cards during a game of Casino. It was unsettling to be scolded by the matriarch of the State of Israel. I felt guilty about it, even though I hadn't done anything wrong. It was my character who was the scoundrel. I may have felt guilty because I never enjoyed Sunday School. Go figure.

Amityville 3-D was probably not the best offer to accept for obvious reasons, but it received the most respectable plaudits of the *Amityville* trilogy. Best of all, by pure coincidence, it gave me the chance to work with Richard Fleischer, the director whose father, Max, had been my mother's boss when she was in her twenties. We coincidentally figured out this connection one day over lunch in Mexico City, where the interior scenes for *Amityville* were being shot. The exterior scenes were filmed later in Tom's River, New Jersey. The Mexican Customs officials took a liking to the wardrobe items they discovered at the airport and simply absconded with them. New wardrobe had to be bought and tailored before filming could continue. We shot several days of "walk-ups" and "drive-ups" and a few scenes outside the house, but it wouldn't take a movie critic to see that people entered the house in different clothing than they were wearing once they were inside. Nevertheless, Richard Fleischer, who directed *Compulsion* and *The Boston Strangler,* was a delight from start to finish, especially when he apologized for having set me on fire during the very last scene. He admitted he had nothing to lose at that point and the effect onscreen would be far more credible than using a double or shooting it from afar. He had the special effects department who, until this point I had survived, fire little pellets of smoldering cork at me until there were coils of smoke coming out of my chest, arms, legs, and so forth. What wasn't counted on was that, as the pellets smoldered, they caught fire to the clothes I was wearing. This was serious. I was beginning to feel the heat, but I didn't hear anyone yell, "Cut!" I fled from the blazing mansion behind me, ran towards the camera and, finally, out of the frame. I was looking for the guy with the fire extinguisher, which, thank God, someone had the good sense to bring along, I didn't need to stick around and see the house burn down, but it did. *Amityville 3-D* raised my profile for a moment, but it was no Mount Rushmore.

My father once told me that fame would come, if it was meant to, in a way that he compared to the splitting of a piece of marble. It wasn't the 738th tap that finally produced the break, but all the other taps that came before it. Being mentioned in a review was one tap, an interview was another, and so on. In other words, becoming famous could take a long time. There was never a defining moment when I felt for sure that it had arrived. I always thought of myself as more of a spear-carrier, that my big break was still on the horizon.

I think I naively believed for many decades that fame itself was the solution to existential insignificance. It was even an antidote to death because, after all, I would still be around whenever they showed my films to future generations, so there was a comfort I enjoyed at the prospect of being unforgettable, even though I was still purely mortal. What a grandiose conceit! I don't believe I can be the first member of SAG-

AFTRA to buy into this idea and as I got older the comfort I got from it receded. Still, it was good while it lasted. As long as TCM is around I can still lay claim to some concept of immortality. And without having to shop for new clothes! Enough! I don't wish to be morbid. But this need to remember the past and reassemble its particulars has always been a focus of my imagination. Maybe I wish I had the chance to do a second "take" and correct some choices I made along the way that weren't always the best options.

Everyone has fantasies about being famous and what it's like to be "known." Saul Bellow, the Pulitzer Prize winning author, said that being "known" doesn't mean much more than being "identified." A dog is known, too. In fact, I took my dog on a television show once and the next day a doorman, who had previously ignored us, called out my dog's name as a friendly greeting. "Hi there, Dexter." he enthused. I saw the same look of confusion cross my dog's face that I've often experienced myself. He was thinking, "Do I know this doorman?"

At one time, I was delighted to be recognized and couldn't wait to answer the many questions put to me by people who had seen my work somewhere, but as it dawned on them that I was a "real person," a "human being" just like them, they began to lose their enthusiasm and even their interest. Rather than stick around to witness their disillusion, I found that it was best to keep moving.

It's best to keep moving for other reasons, too. For instance, a guy on the street once asked me for money. When I told him I had nothing on me, he looked me in the eye and said he would never watch my television show again. I told him it had been cancelled anyway, and I moved on. I got into a heated argument with another guy on Fifth Avenue who insisted that I was Wayne Rogers. I told him who I really was, but he said he never heard of me. It infuriated me that he wouldn't believe that I was me! Of course, it's nice to get a good table, to be treated courteously, and especially to receive smiles from strangers. They know that I know that they know who I am. But fame, as someone much wiser than me once said, arrests life around it. The world looks harder at a celebrity than at most passers-by. The celebrity doesn't always see life going on around him because, too often, it's looking back at him.

Some people approach me with such familiarity that I'm sure they're someone I've met before, or perhaps they're even a part of my large family—I've got a lot of cousins. I've had lengthy conversations with people whose identity I was afraid to question for fear of offending them. "Do I know you, or are you just a fan?" is the question I'm desperate to ask, and sometimes I can't help but just ask it. The result can be confusing if both of us have made a mistake. I might just as well be Wayne Rogers talking to a total stranger on Fifth Avenue.

My most peculiar experience is being "captioned," my word for what happens when someone I pass in the street announces to no one in particular, "Tony Roberts." It's as if he were flipping the pages of a school primer and has come across a familiar image. I don't now whether to say, "You're right," or "Thank you," or nothing at all, or "Bingo." He's not evaluating me. He's already flipped to the next page and couldn't care less if I respond or not. He's paid me the compliment of knowing my name, but at the same time, he's let me know exactly what its worth to him: not much. It's a perspective I try to keep in mind.

My own perspective was expanded by working with George Burns in the film *18 Again!* I was playing his son and the director wanted another "take."

"Sorry, George! The camera had a little problem." he said.

He was referring to a slight jiggle, or a miscalculation of focus.

After he walked away George leaned into my ear and whispered, "Can you believe it? I'm ninety-two years-old and the *camera* has a problem!"

He flashed me his infamous wry smile. He was so glad to be alive and working. He was too frail to shoot all day, but he was always prepared to do his job and enjoyed a martini when he was finished. He was a great role model.

I've never played a brute, except in an Off-Broadway play for the Manhattan Theatre Club, which was, unfortunately, not well received. I made my first entrance of the night in the third act. I didn't have to get to the theatre until nine o'clock, which was great in some ways, but I missed the schmoozing and fun routine of everything that happens backstage after half-hour is called. I made my entrance and after a few lines of dialogue proceeded to violently assault two women, Jane Alexander and Shirley Knight, who had offended me in some way. I don't remember how. The New Yorker review said, "What's a nice Jewish boy like Tony Roberts doing in a play like this?"

As an actor, I didn't make a good thug. I could only be tough if I thought I was Burt Lancaster, Kirk Douglas, or Gregory Peck, which I had done so well to keep the bad guys away from me when I was in the Army that I was put in charge of my platoon as an acting Staff Sergeant. I actually broke up a fight once between two guys in a hallway outside my room (yes, I had my own room—I was the Sergeant!). One of them held a bayonet, and the other was swinging a rifle butt at him. I stood in the doorway and had no choice. It was up to me to stop it. "Wait a minute you guys," doing my best Lancaster imitation. "What do you boys think you're doing?" At this point in *From Here to Eternity*, Lancaster breaks a whiskey bottle and threatens to use it against one of the assailants. We didn't have a bottle so I had to do without it, nor could I say his line, "Ain't nobody gonna do nothin'." but the two of them froze where they stood. They were stunned, but also grateful. "Now put those things down and go back to bed." I growled. "We gotta get up in a few hours!" I went back to my room. "And keep it down, I'd like to catch some sleep tonight!" I'm sure those sentences were peppered with dirty words because in basic training that's the only way you can avoid seeming privileged, or upper class, or even middle class. What you want to be is no class, just dangerous; just "don't fuck with me" class. After I closed the door it took me several moments to catch my breath, let alone catch any sleep. Had I done that? Wow, and no one was even there to see it. *That's* how an actor thinks!

An actor thinks of himself as a character in a story, which has a beginning, a middle, and an end. Having only our own past as a reference, we invent imaginary lives for the characters we get cast to play. Otherwise, God forbid, we would have to be our own naked selves out there in front of all those strangers and lights. Yet people still ask, "How do you remember all those lines?" We remember them because they are our lifeline to the story we have made up in our heads that links them to the purpose, at any given moment, of the character we are playing. Burt Lancaster taught me how to handle that moment in the hall outside my room as much as anything that ever happened to me in real life. I learned how to understand life at the movies. That's where things made sense.

While I was doing *Promises, Promises* in Los Angeles my agent convinced someone at the Walt Disney Studio to take a look at me. I was offered a supporting role in *The Million Dollar Duck*. It wasn't exactly *On the Waterfront*, but I was glad to get into the picture business any way I could. In the first scene, I had to crawl on the grounds of an enormous enclosure that reeked of excrement worthy of the monkey house in Central Park. There were a few hundred ducks in my path and I barked at them, as called for in the script, to encourage their reproductive impulses, which caused them to produce eggs made of pure gold. Really.

"What happened to Shakespeare?" I thought. How is this thing going to turn out? I didn't have to be Henry V, but this was the other extreme. When I was given my first tour of the Disney lot in Burbank, the director showed me a set of drawings they had made of me in various poses and expressions like a comic strip. "That's you," he said, pointing to a character whose hair and figure resembled my own. "Do you see how surprised you are in that shot?" Indeed, my illustrated representation had his mouth agape and his eyebrows raised. I was being shown the actual expressions I was expected to produce once the cameras started rolling. The entire movie had been storyboarded like this. The executives at Disney left no room for mistakes or fuzzy interpretations. They knew, before the actors had been cast, how the film would be edited and where the laughs would fall. All I had to do was follow the dots.

I was horrified. It's considered bush-league to suggest a specific line-reading for an actor, basically telling an actor, "say the line like this," except as a last resort. Some actors even believe they can never find the spontaneity of their performance if it's been spoon-fed to them this way, regardless of how well-intended the spooner. This was something even beyond a line-reading, not just "say it like this" but also "make this face!" But, this was my first picture, so I didn't complain. They wanted to leave as little to chance as possible in this highly collaborative medium. The mistakes were too financially unacceptable. *The Million Dollar Duck* made a lot of money, but it sure was a stinker to make.

Working on the Walt Disney lot was particularly surreal. The streets had names like Mickey Mouse Lane, or Donald Duck Avenue, and the studio executives had hired a small musical ensemble to play familiar favorites on the lawn as their employees strolled to lunch. I even got to dine at Walt's own table in the well-appointed commissary as a guest of the film's producers. There were four of us around a beautiful corner table and a place was fully set for the dearly departed Walt in front of his empty chair, now customary. It was all very reverential. I almost expected him to show up.

The first film was the toughest to get, but the second followed quickly on its heels. Neil Simon gave his approval to Bob Evans at Paramount and I was cast in *Star Spangled Girl* with Sandy Duncan. The picture didn't hang around very long, as they say. I was becoming concerned about my gravitas, or lack thereof. I needed some respect.

When Woody's films kicked in, they brought with them a degree of respectability that I otherwise would not have enjoyed. And surely working for Sydney Lumet in *Serpico* and *Just Tell Me What You Want* increased the value of my stock in a way that led to other opportunities. I did everything I could to keep the ball rolling and auditioned whenever asked to. I made seven pilots in all, and a few of them made it on the air, but none turned out to be hits. Maybe that wasn't such a bad thing because, although a hit television series was the only way to become a millionaire in this business, it could also take its toll on the soul. It creates a dilemma on a weekly basis. The product, at least most of the time, is mediocre, demographically conceived, and the result of many hands, from the credited writer to the network lawyers who must protect themselves against the reactions of offended fans. In addition, there are stringent time limits imposed on casts and crews due to the costs of production. Product is expensive, so most of the time you're doing poor material. Even worse, you're doing it quickly.

I starred in *Rosetti and Ryan* for NBC, who hoped that it would unseat its chief rival in a highly valued Sunday night time slot. It didn't. I was to learn that we were cancelled from the security guard at the gate of Universal Studios, on my way to work for the twelfth episode. My personal belongings had been removed from my trailer as it was needed for another show, and I could collect my "stuff" from The Tower. The Tower was the tall glass office building that loomed over the lot. All the "suits" were there, high above the factory workers toiling in the hulking sound stages down below. Big decisions always came from The Tower. My previously well-featured headshot was removed from the commissary.

In a similar circumstance, I was sent on a publicity tour by CBS a few years later to promote a show called *The Four Seasons* written by Alan Alda. I had just finished raving about the show on the New Orleans CBS affiliate station and was at the airport en route to my next scheduled promotion. It happened to be my mother's birthday, and I had time to call her before my flight took off. She gave me the news of the cancelation during our long-distance phone call. She'd already heard about it on the radio. News travels fast.

The moment I was out of work, I hated being asked what I was "doing," read: working on. It's the most dreaded question an actor can be asked, but it comes with the territory. What follows is an excerpt from an interview on NBC with Gene Shalit:

> GS: Tony Roberts is in the hit Broadway musical *They're Playing Our Song* co-starring Lucie Arnaz. He is about to open a movie with Ali

McGraw and Alan King called *Just Tell Me What You Want.* He is currently in a radio mystery series. Next week he'll be in a TV movie on CBS. He was in the Academy Award winning movie *Annie Hall* and it makes me tired just thinking of everything you do. Why do you work so hard, Tony? Don't you ever take a vacation?

TR: No. I crack under leisure. I need to have a lot of things to do. I'm very compulsive.

GS: Is it fear? Do you think nobody will love you if you go away?

TR: I'm afraid they won't know me when I come back.

GS: When's the last time you had a vacation? Can you remember it?

TR: Actors don't take vacations, you know. We just become unemployed.

As I made more films I became more aware of how different it was to act in front of a camera than to act in a theatre. Onstage, one needs to project so that the last row of the balcony is as easy a place to understand what's going on as the front row of the orchestra, but it has to appear that you are speaking in a natural tone to a person only a few feet away. When you speak lines on a movie set the old pros will tell you, "If the sound engineer doesn't ask you to speak up, then you're already speaking loudly enough." In film work it's all about NOT projecting anything except the part you can't control and the part that happens despite your best efforts to control it. Any projection will register as false. The camera is so close and what it sees is so magnified that a good screen actor will let a thought drift across his eyes and know that he has just spoken volumes.

As for Los Angeles, I never really felt comfortable there. I enjoyed walking the streets of Manhattan and running into people. There was always a sense of "now" for me in the crowded city, more than there ever was in the empty streets of Beverly Hills. Despite twice having signed six-month leases, I never put down real roots there. I considered myself lucky that I could still find work in the Broadway theatre, and I was blessed to be busy. I played the Cary Grant role in a successful revival of *Arsenic and Old Lace*, and did a lengthy stint in *They're Playing Our Song*. I liked doing eight shows a week. I had also gained some attention from being in some good films like *The Taking of Pelham One Two Three* and a picture called *Le Sauvage* starring Catherine Deneuve and Yves Montand.

Spring, 1975

My poorest subject in high school, with the exception of Math, which I hated, was French. I was at an immediate disadvantage because my early education was at the School of Ethical Culture which espoused the theory that too much discipline diminished creativity. Thus, by the time I reached the fourth grade I had no reading skills, and spent a good deal of time wrestling in the halls, or staring into space. I never learned proper grammar. My parents transferred me to a public school and, with the help of a private tutor, I eventually caught up with the rest of the fifth grade.

Imagine then, how extraordinary it was to be asked, almost begged, by the great

French film star Yves Montand, to speak his lines into a tape recorder so that he would seem more proficient in English to American audiences. I was happy to do it and flattered that he had asked me. We were in Venezuela shooting a romantic comedy. My part was all in French and I spent two weeks, at their request, in Caracas working with a teacher to perfect my pronunciation. I played a jilted lover who chases Deneuve throughout the film because she stole a valuable painting from my office. Naturally, Montand ended up catching her, and I ended up with a damaged painting.

One afternoon, as we waited for the camera to get ready, Yves waxed philosophically for a few actors standing nearby. "We're very lucky to be actors," he said. "After all, we get to play games, like children, and pretend in make-believe. What could be more fun? And even better, we get paid to do it! That is why we need to take our work very seriously. We need to prepare, to know our lines, and always be ready to work. But…," at this point he clearly wanted to make a point. "Don't ever take yourself too seriously. That's when you go off the track." I've always wondered if his observations had been prompted by something he thought I needed to hear. At any rate, I've never forgotten what he said. I could be pretty serious in those days, especially since I was working with the man many referred to as "the Sinatra of Europe." *Le Sauvage* won a César Award, the French equivalent of an Oscar. It was called *Lovers Like Us* when it was released in English in the United States. I had to dub my part back into English, but on the screen my lips were speaking French. Tricky, but not impossible.

One evening during the filming, I was invited to join these internationally famous superstars along with Charles Aznavour for dinner in a fancy restaurant following a performance of his one-man show. After the concert, the four of us were sitting at a table getting ready to order when eight American tourists were suddenly standing at my elbow. I must mention here that as friendly and polite as my three French friends were I was sure that they had never heard of me, or anything I had ever done. These travelers from

Oklahoma recognized me from *The Edge of Night*, ten years earlier.

"You're Lee Pollack!" they squealed, and were beside themselves with excitement. They had no clue as to who the other people at the table were, but asked me to sign their menus. I considered introducing them to the three superstars, but feared that even these fans from the hinterlands might not be impressed and I would have to promote them, as well as introduce them. I chose to sign my name and get it over with as quickly as possible. The three stars looked on in stony silence. I think they felt embarrassed not to have known that I had ever been seen enough to be recognized by anybody. I was treated with a newfound respect on the set, but had to start picking up my own checks after that.

Sometimes, big stars can't hide no matter where they happen to be. I was staying in a hotel in Beverly Hills during the making of a television movie when I sauntered into the steam room with a towel around my waist. It was difficult to see through the mist, but I found the steps to the tiled bleachers and took a seat. There was only one other person in there sitting about halfway up. It was Tony Curtis. I had never met him, and didn't want to invade his privacy, but, after a while, I couldn't resist. I had played his role from *Some Like it Hot* when it was adapted into the musical *Sugar*. The role required a lot of time in drag. I didn't speak for several minutes, and he was oblivious to my presence. Finally, I said, "Mr. Curtis, it's impossible for me to sit here and not point out that you and I are the only two actors in the world who have ever played the part of Josephine!" It took him a moment to put everything together, but then we had a good laugh and a good sweat.

Later that day, I ran into Martin Balsam on Rodeo Drive. He was a fine actor and, in the way that professionals do, we recognized each other and stopped to chat. For just a moment Rodeo Drive felt like Seventh Avenue. I told him how well things were going for me and he said, "Naturally, it's your time!"

What did he mean by that? He said it without a trace of bitterness, and I was certainly happy to believe that it was "my time," but it doesn't take a genius to realize that time itself is not only passing, but fleeting. The message was that my "time" would eventually come to an end. He was telling me to "smell the roses" and he was right. The networks and studios spend fortunes to find out who their audience knows and how they feel about them. Actors are given mathematical ratings that affect their negotiating ability. The longer the period of time an actor stays out of the limelight, the lower his numbers fall. Networks and studios subscribe to services who provide them with such statistics.

Along these lines, if one is lucky enough to be cast in a big role in a feature film, it's necessary to guarantee the studio that you are in good health. To accomplish this, you are examined by a doctor acceptable to the insurance companies. They offer policies to indemnify the studio in the event one of their stars becomes ill and can't finish the picture. The doctor I saw with some frequency during my good years was a very warm and genial fellow. I once told him I was glad to be seeing him because I hadn't worked for a while. I had been in one of the aforementioned valleys of an actor's career. The kindly doctor put down his stethoscope and, sounding like the famous doorman in *Grand Hotel*, said, "You know, I see them all. Everyone has to come here, the 'great' and the 'not so great.' They come and they go, but let me tell you, there's no one in Hollywood for whom the phone hasn't stopped ringing." I found that idea oddly reassuring.

Because of my visibility at the time, an agent once booked me to speak to a convention of automobile salesman who had won a free trip to Rome for outselling their competitors. I would travel first class and regale a group of two hundred, or so, about my passion for the importance of meaningful theatre. They would also give me ten thousand dollars. The salesmen and I all got off the long overnight flight together and were whisked away to a five-star hotel where, jet lagged and dragging our luggage, we were assembled in a large banquet hall which now resembled a high school auditorium. Ten minutes later, having launched into a fifty minute presentation I realized that this was a disaster. By the time I mentioned Alvina

Krause a good number of them had their eyes closed and were trying to catch up on some sleep. The ones who stayed awake were dumbstruck because of the subject at hand. What the hell did they care about the death of Chekovian theatre on University campuses? I couldn't buy a laugh. Even Gregory Peck couldn't have saved it.

I realize that there doesn't seem to be a clearly marked ending to this particular chapter. It has an amorphous feel about it. Perhaps that's because the "Get Me Tony Roberts!!" phase doesn't turn into the "Get Me a Young Tony Roberts!" phase overnight. Gradually you're offered roles less and less as someone's son and more often asked to play someone's father (and ultimately, if your luck holds out, someone's grandpa). This clarification evolves over a period of time that is impossible to pinpoint. My career never stopped dead in its tracks as I got older, because I had diversified my ambitions to such an extent that there was always something within my grasp. It might be a voice-over commercial, a chance to do a classic in a regional theatre, a performance at a benefit, or even a chance to direct something, which I did with a play written by Charles Grodin at the Vineyard Theatre in Manhattan. I didn't really slow down as Phase Three became Phase Four, but I had to readjust my self-image. It's like trying to watch the hands of a clock move. It's impossible to see it happen, but after a few minutes, the time has changed. I was becoming aware that playing Henry V was not going to happen, at least not a young Henry V, however I still had a few Broadway runs ahead of me and continued to be active in films and television. There was still much rewarding work to do in Phase Four, and even in Phase Five, but that comes later. No complaints.

Nathaniel Trochman, Fanny Naft, and me.

Fanny Naft

Nathaniel Trochman

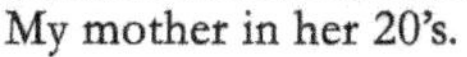
My mother in her 20's.

Me, age 5.

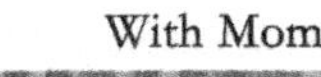
With Mom.

With Dad.

(L to R, front): Uncle Bob, Dad, Mom, Herman Finklestein
(L to R, back): Grandma Fanny, me, Nancy, Ann Finklestein

My sister, Nancy.

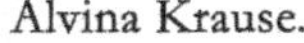

Alvina Krause.

My first headshot.

My Broadway debut. *Something About a Soldier,* 1962. (L to R): Sid Raymond, Ralph Meeker, Sal Mineo, and me. Photo by Friedman-Abeles/© Billy Rose Theatre Division, The New York Library for the Performing Arts.

(L): With Penny Fuller in *Barefoot in the Park*, 1965.

Photo by Friedman-Abeles/© Billy Rose Theatre Division, The New York Library for the Performing Arts.

(R): With Lucie Arnaz in *They're Playing Our Song*, 1980.

Photo by Martha Swope/© Billy Rose Theatre Division, The New York Library for the Performing Arts.

Annie Hall, 1977. ©MGM

Jerome Robbins' Broadway, 1990.

Playing Hamlet, 1972.

Promises, Promises (Broadway), 1970.
Photo by Martha Swope/© Billy Rose Theatre Division, The New York Library for the Performing Arts.

With Bernadette Peters and Carol Burnett on the set of *The Carol Burnett Show.*

Sugar, 1972.

L to R: Robert Morse, Elaine Joyce, and me.

Photo by Martha Swope/© Billy Rose Theatre Division, The New York Library for the Performing Arts.

On the set of *Popcorn*, 1991.

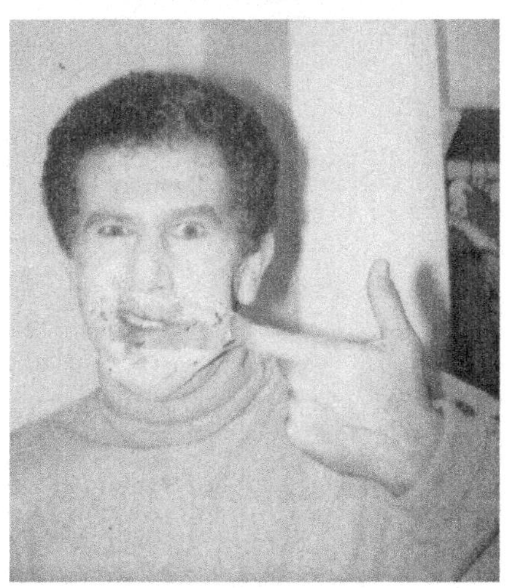

Dad and me.

Pitching at Shea Stadium in a charity event.

With Julie Andrews in *Victor/Victoria*, 1995.

My daughter, Nicole.

Jerome Robbins

It's an established ritual, when you are lucky enough to tour with a show in a foreign country, that you make yourself available for various photo ops and interviews. Such was the case when *Jerome Robbins' Broadway* was being promoted by Japanese journalists who had been invited to New York by the Shubert Organization. The cast was assembled in a shuttered Joe Allen's Restaurant on West 46th Street.

"Where you from, Tony?" one of them asked.

"New York City." I said.

"Yes, but where you really from? Where your parents from?"

"New York City." I reply. "My parents were born in New York City, too."

"Okay, then where were grandparents born?"

"Russia."

"Oh, so you Russian."

"No," I say, fearing I'm about to cause an international incident. "I'm American."

It was difficult for them to accept the logic of such a concept. It wasn't possible for anyone to become Japanese, unless they were, so how could someone from Russia claim to be American? I wasn't going to argue. I was already having trouble understanding the translators.

Jerome Robbins' Broadway ran for two years and was an anthology of the best showstoppers that Broadway ever produced. I was a replacement in the role that won Jason Alexander a Tony Award. The whole project was a dream come true. Here I was for over fourteen months, including the Japanese tour, standing in front of the finest fifty dancers to be found in the land, introducing the landmark creations spanning twenty-five years of Broadway's Golden Age. I changed costumes at least twelve times during each show as I sang and danced my way through almost all the numbers I had rehearsed in my room when I was still in elementary school. How great it was to be the guy with the mop swabbing the deck at the opening of *On the*

Town just before the entire company leaps on the stage to sing *New York, New York*. It was a vivid moment I can still recall as I fell in love with musicals. I was too old to be one of those recruits, but it was my line that cued the lights and the orchestra and the dozens of sailors who suddenly filled the stage.

"What time is it now, Bud?"

"Six o'clock, will ya!!!" And then all hell broke loose.

There was a cast ritual practiced whenever a new performer joined the company of *Jerome Robbins' Broadway*. On the new initiate's opening night, the entire company would gather onstage at the five-minute call and form a circle. A blindfold was placed over the head of the innocent and he was spun around by a hundred hands in circles until his legs were wobbling beneath him. This baptism, as it were, was timed so that the blindfold would be removed at exactly the moment the curtain went up, revealing the full cast facing front as the first words are spoken, welcoming the audience and explaining what they're about to see. On my first day in the show, it was me who had to speak those first words. I wasn't sure if I was even facing the right direction. I can't believe that such a wicked prank was ever invented, but I had nothing to say about it. Having passed the test it was, of course, great fun to look forward to the next poor soul forced to undergo this audacious trespass on an artist's most private and sacred moment.

"Get over it!" I said to myself. "At least you didn't fall into the pit, and you didn't break any bones."

Robbins himself, despite his reputation as a tyrannical perfectionist, was extremely courteous to me during the time I spent in his presence. His notes were direct, specific, and helpful. Preparing the New York company for a Los Angeles run, he could get a little worked up.

"Why are you standing on stage center?" he yelled at me from the first row of the theatre. "Stage center is the dullest place on the stage. It has no tension to it. You can stand six feet to the left of it, or six feet to the right of it, but never just stand dead center. Who, in heaven's name, ever told you to do that?" He was close to a tantrum.

"You did. Yesterday."

"Oh. Well, don't ever do it again. It's a terrible idea."

That was as angry as he ever got with me, but he had brought two dancers, a stage manager, and a pianist to tears, and it was only the first week of rehearsal. The cast was so afraid of him that rehearsals were often torturous. He ate his lunch from a brown paper bag sitting on a hard stool near the apron of the stage. He seldom exchanged the niceties of friendly behavior at rehearsals, although if you passed him on the street, he would treat you as your favorite uncle might.

"Why are you always picking on me?" demanded a dancer with the spirit to challenge his bullying. "I'm doing the steps as well as anybody. I'm never late and I'm always in the right spot. Why do you have a problem with me?" This kind of backtalk was a rare instance of courage that completely stumped him.

"Well…" he muttered. "I don't know… maybe it's because… you're short."

"That's not my fault, and there's nothing I can do about it. After all, *you* cast me knowing I was short. Either fire me or leave me alone!"

After that, she became his favorite cast member.

There were so many different dancers in a variety of costumes that it took forever to learn who everybody was. Most of the ensemble wore at least six different costumes and were sporting various wigs, as well. There were three guys named Glenn and four Marys. There were so many people changing clothes with the assistance of dressers and make-up artists that there wasn't a foot of backstage that hadn't been converted into a quick-change booth. There was even a quick-change booth halfway up the side aisle, which had been converted from a public coat room. These brief intervals, spent in crowded quarters with the same cast and crew eight times a week, gave birth to the best laughter I have ever known, and every guffaw had to be suppressed. It was like an improvised running sitcom less than five minutes in duration, but filled with the minutiae of typical offstage buzz and show-business gossip. I looked forward to these gag fests more than anything else in the day. These five-minute respites were too short, of course. They could have been an hour longer, just to allow for laughter.

"We have a sighting!" exclaimed two or three cast members as they tumbled into the wings at the halfway mark of the first act. Indeed, the entire company directed their gaze to the eighth row, center aisle seat, where Jerome Robbins scribbled notes on a yellow legal pad that he would deliver to the company after the show. The pallor of the cast went from rosy red to ashen as everyone struggled to give their absolute all for the remainder of the show. Afterwards, he wasn't displeased with me. I was told by the regulars I should consider that lack of displeasure a tremendous compliment.

The most surprising aspect about my experience with Robbins was how similar in approach to the work he was to my old mentor Alvina Krause. They were each hoping to startle an audience by showing them the truth of something transcendent. They were both determined to create it or capture it, as if it were the "elixir of life." When Robbins recreated the *West Side Story* sequence, which ended the first act of *Jerome Robbins' Broadway*, he declared to the cast on the first day of what would turn out to be a five-month-long rehearsal period, that the dancers cast as Sharks were not allowed any social engagement whatsoever with anyone cast as a Jet, and vice versa. This created an almost tribal animosity before they ever got their sneakers on. Act One of *Jerome Robbins' Broadway* was so dynamic that in Japan, half the audience did not return after intermission. It was said that the audience had really only come to see the *West Side Story* sequence in the first place because they believed it to be the pinnacle of Robbins' contribution to the musical theatre genre. At any rate, I never missed watching the last forty minutes of the first act from the wings downstage left, keeping as far out of the way of the exiting dancers as possible. Three or four of them were always being attended to on the floor behind me as they grabbed at their joints in pain. There was no way to perform this number without the element of risk. There were six swings, or subs, who filled in for the injured, each of them bringing into the mix a new pattern of time and space all their own, thus increasing the chances for collisions and concussions, but the fight sequences had undeniable impact.

Similar to Ms. Krause, Robbins wanted me to reach beyond my own self-prescribed limitations. He forced me to trust in my imagination. When rehearsing the Tevye dream sequence from *Fiddler on the Roof*, he actually got down on the floor next to me and acted out the fear and trembling that Tevye is supposed to be going through, then he pleaded for me to express my feelings at least five times more demonstratively than I otherwise would. Once encouraged to explore this new realm of "belief," it is like tasting heaven. You can find your way back there again and again eight times a week if you're lucky enough to meet someone with the patience to take you there. Both Alvina Krause and Jerome Robbins did that for me.

During the run in Tokyo, a false front tooth fell out of my mouth in the middle of my last line as Tevye. I was downstage right, lit by a bright spotlight, and I heard a ping from the boards as I began to speak. My tongue also found a huge gap in my upper front gum. I had lost a crown, and an expensive one, too. I couldn't just leave it there. I would never find it during the scene change. What if it should get kicked into the orchestra pit by one of the dancers? I decided to pick it up in front of sixteen hundred people, who probably wouldn't know what I was doing. I swooped it off the floor, spun upstage for a moment, checked to see that it was facing the right direction and jammed the crown into my upper gum. I didn't want to lose it again.

"And tho…" intending to say "so…" "they were married and the people of Anatevka withed them every happineth!"

I could hear the cascades of laughter from my peers as the story made its way up the stairs to the dressing rooms. The joke was that I had proven myself too cheap to stay in character, deciding instead not to have to buy a new dental implant.

"But I didn't break character," I protested. "Tevye would have done the same thing!"

And so would Nachman Trochman. Tho there!

I was in that show for fourteen months and bonded with dozens of wonderful people I would otherwise never have known, but I think it's that way with most casts, if not all. I would have continued for a while longer were it not for an injury I suffered during the most hilarious number in the show. We called it "The Doors" number because it was a chase involving the whole cast, who had to enter and exit an absurd number of times through twelve identical doors. I should mention that this was all happening at lightning speed and in time with specific musical cues. In short, a person could get killed. To my knowledge, no one died, but many were shaken up at times and everybody took that number very seriously. You could never be sure if the door you were waiting to enter might not be the door about to slam in your face. I was required to execute a balletic leap called a "cecchetti changement." It sounds like a sports car, but after fourteen months of doing them, my gears were shot (I'm sorry for that one, but I couldn't help it).

Jerome Robbins

I left the company and said hello to a double hernia operation. No big deal.

Risky Business

Larry Blyden, a wonderful actor with a long list of Broadway credits, always posted a list of his "rules" on the callboard on the first day of rehearsal. They were funny dos and don'ts that applied to any cast about to start a new project. There were twelve rules, as I recall, but every third one was the same. "Save Your Money!" Anyone who has survived in show business knows that this is good advice.

In addition to the usual ups and downs of any career, actors are often victimized by unscrupulous money managers. Thus it was that I was stripped financially clean just as my daughter was about to start college. I was stunned to discover that I was not only dead broke, (ironically the title of an independent film I was cast in during this period) but also in deep debt to the IRS. All of this came as a complete shock and for the first time in my life, I had less than two dollars in my pocket. That was not enough to pay for the least expensive piece of fried chicken at the local take-out joint near my home. It was very humbling. It took me nearly a decade to recover. I was saved in no small part through the great efforts of friends and honest accountants, but I was forced to accept the kind of work I otherwise wouldn't have. One such project was *Popcorn,* and I tried to make the best of it. It wasn't a great picture, but it did receive respectable notices from both the New York and Los Angeles Times.

Popcorn was a special effects picture. Kingston, Jamaica has many things to its advantage, but it's an odd choice as a site in which to shoot this particular picture. There are absolutely no exterior or interior shots that require anything that relates to this climate zone, its topography, or the culture of the Caribbean. Kingston also has no studios or, in fact, any film industry whatsoever.

The crew was composed of some extremely reserved and distinguished types, mostly out of London and Toronto. When one lingered near the camera, the accents stretched from broad Cockney, with its rhyming slang and British war movie flavor, to the more elegant and aristocratic sentences spoken by the esteemed cinematographer, Mr.

Ron Taylor of *Gandhi* fame, no less. The special effects constructionists were a group from Italy and their English was about as good as my Italian, which was not very. Finally, there were the Jamaicans themselves who comprised about seventy-five percent of the crew. Their speech was almost entirely made up of Patois. The only words in patois I could understand were Marley and Ganja.

We were shooting a horror movie, also intended to be a spoof of the genre. The lobby of the movie house, which served as our set, was decorated with actual placards, posters, and photographs from a broad range of horror films proclaiming themselves to be the ultimate source of terror. As I waited for my next shot, I studied this gallery of mostly forgettable schlock and wondered whether the picture I was making was better or worse than most of them.

We were shooting a sequence which required four-and-a-half hours in the make-up chair for a shot that lasted about eight-seconds. In it, I pull a rubber mask away from my face which has been so subtly molded to my features that it was difficult to know where my real face began and the mask ended. We did a take and it went well. We did a second one, for safety, and during this take, my left ear accidentally ripped off in my hand and, with great improvisational spontaneity, I uttered a surprised, "Oh!" The director said, "Cut!" The take became known as the Vincent Van Gogh scene, and one of the special effects people added a few dabs of blood to the ear and slipped it into the biscuit basket at lunch.

A different torture faced the leading lady. Her role called for her to be entombed like a mummy and wheeled around in a coffin in the villain's laboratory. No one knew that this particular actress suffered from acute claustrophobia. As the camera rolled, she broke down in a fit of tears while the crew stood by, helplessly. The picture had to have the shot and it got made.

In one sequence, my character, who is not really my character at this point in the story because my character is dead, is tied by a rope to a beautiful woman. We kiss. As our lips part, a piece of my face comes off in the woman's mouth. Cut to me. I look ghoulish. I am actually eating my own face. She recoils, tries to escape. Cut.

Brief though it was, this scene required two hours in the make-up chair each time it was shot. Three experts with sponges and brushes dabbed latex, grease paint, and various adhesives on my face until I was completely grossed out by the sight of myself. After the make-up was applied, I made my way up a narrow stairway leading to the high catwalk above the stage where this scene would be shot. I don't like heights. When I got to the center of the catwalk, I was tied and glued on the spot to my counterpart whose lips, once the director yelled, "Action!" would supposedly pull the flesh away from my… well, my skeleton, I suppose. We did this procedure five times as two cameras shot simultaneously. It took a day-and-a-half. After one attempt, the camera operator, whose eye is the only one that actually sees the moment when all the preproduction work ends and post production begins, said, "It looks through the lens as though the little strips of latex have been neatly snipped by a manicurist's scissors," which was exactly true, so it was off the catwalk, down the stairway, and back to the drawing board.

What saved the day was our special effect artist's idea to pre-glue little strips of flesh-colored latex to our chin and lips just before the camera rolled. The strips were then coated with KY Jelly in order to look really repulsive on the screen. We learned to call these strips "nernies." One time the nernies broke too soon and we had to start over. Another time, they didn't break at all until my entire prosthetic face came off in the actress' mouth.

Yuuuuucchhh.

Meanwhile, I imagined my agent resting near his pool, content with the thought that he'd provided me with a job and that I was finally off his back for a while.

The final scene was shot in an old movie house in Kingston, which was once an elegant opera house. I was strapped to a high scaffold suspended just below the ceiling of the theatre. I am to be impaled by the proboscis of a twelve-foot, eighty-pound mosquito whose eyes pulse and whose tail fills with blood as I am sucked dry and pushed off the scaffold to splatter like a pancake on the floor below.

Each time this sequence is shot — and it is shot repeatedly because the director wants to show it from every angle; close-up, long shot, from my point of view, from the mosquito's point of view—I am continuously re-impaled, as it were. The blood from the puncture has to be reapplied because it keeps drying and the mosquito has to be emptied and repositioned. This is no small feat when you consider that it has been made to speed around cables up to forty miles per hour while flapping its wings. It is especially difficult if the people operating it are speaking three different languages. On the first day, the Italians missed a signal and the huge insect crashed into the camera, scattering the crew in all directions and setting us back half a day.

As I lay there, hoping that the scaffold was not made by the same guy who sold me my sandals at the hotel, I remembered Sigourney Weaver in *Aliens*, defending herself against a host of demonic creatures. She triumphed over them and had the satisfaction of receiving an Academy Award nomination.

I, on the other hand, had to die halfway through the picture, a victim of the worst mosquito bite in the history of the world. I wouldn't be writing any Oscar speeches.

New York City Opera

October, 1991

"How would you like to play one of the leads in *Brigadoon* in the New York City Opera's production at Lincoln Center?"

"Are you kidding?" I say.

"They've asked for you. Beverly Sills herself! It means you'll miss pilot season and there's no money in it. What do you think?"

"No question. Absolutely. I have to do it. I would pay them."

"I agree. Congratulations."

And so began one of the happiest and most interesting episodes of my career. I was to discover later that mine was a non-singing role, a detail which disappointed me at first, but later on, after hearing the singers, I considered it a blessing. I wasn't very familiar with the book of *Brigadoon*. I'd seen the film version, but that wasn't exactly authentic to the original. It turns out that I was to play the Van Johnson role. Once I accepted the job, I got a hold of the script and saw what was what. It was the wrong way to do things when choosing a project, but this was special.

The script shocked me. *How could this work?* At first reading, it seemed corny and my character unredeemable. He was a drunk, a man who resisted the faiths on which the fable was based. Had I made a mistake? Had I been caught in a bluff with no part to play? I was worried.

The State Theatre at Lincoln Center (Now the David H. Koch Theatre) is the one on the left as you face the fountain, and it's an intimidating structure. To get backstage, one must traverse the coldest, most wind-swept corner of New York City. West 62nd Street and Columbus Avenue is an open space, as spaces go in New York, and one often gets hurled inside the stage door by a giant gust of wind. Once there, you are facing a man in uniform behind a counter at the top of some stairs.

It's the *Barney Miller Show*, I think. I must've made a wrong turn somewhere. But no, after a brief interrogation as to my purposes, I am ushered through a door and told to follow the black squares in the linoleum pattern on the floor. They will lead me to the wardrobe department for my first fitting. I haven't even met the cast yet, but this procedure is not unusual. It takes time to make costumes.

I have never been one for following instructions, so I take this opportunity to wander off the beaten path of black linoleum squares and begin to explore the building. It doesn't take long to be lost in the labyrinth of hallways and staircases which all seem alike and go on forever. There are crates lining the walls with the titles of operas and ballets stamped on them. They provide the only clue as to which hallway one is in at any given moment. After being led around in circles for a while, I began to recognize that I'd been to a certain spot before. At the end of one dead end, I cautiously opened a door a few inches and my curiosity was exquisitely rewarded. I was eavesdropping on a rehearsal by the New York City Ballet Company of George Gershwin's *Concerto in F*, a ballet I have seen from the audience, and a piece of music I have loved and listened to *ad infinitum* since I was a boy. I could have stood there forever. I couldn't believe I was working in the same building. After all, sometimes when you rehearse in this business, you open a door and discover people getting ready to shoot an Alpo commercial. I had arrived.

The first rehearsal for *Brigadoon* was held around a table in a sterile concrete cell in the bowels of the theatre. There, on folding chairs, were the principal players and designers of this brand new production, made possible by Lawrence Wien. He's a man who loves musical theatre and who offered the opportunity to Ms. Sills and Company to produce a season of revivals that would do justice to Broadway's claims of immortality. This production would be the first of three that would receive his financial support. It was Ms. Sills' idea to use two different casts for the leads. I, however, would play all performances. That would mean playing with different performers from night to night.

I have had some experience with long runs and of trying to maintain a constancy from night to night that is rooted in exact predictables like the clarity of a setup line, the timing of a cross, the stillness of the stage, the intensity of the interplay, and so forth. Under this new circumstance, I thought I would never accumulate enough repetition from night to night to develop a pattern, to discover the best possible scenario in order to get the laugh or make the scene work.

I began to discover that there is a benefit to double casting, at least from where I stood. I got to rehearse everything twice as much as everybody else! I was also forced to abandon the idea of "setting" anything.

On a table nearby was a miniature model of the set, to give us an idea of where we were going to be living onstage. Desmond Healy, the designer, demonstrated how things came on and got off, and showed us his costume sketches on large cardboards. They were ready for museum display, even then.

The actors were introduced by our director, Gerald Friedman. "I saw this show as a young man and never forgot it." he said. "To me, there is great magic and wonder in it, and I want it to affect people in the same way it affected me. I think it can work. I believe in it."

During a coffee break, one of the staff took me through a door at the end of a short hallway. There, below me, was the stage of the State Theatre. I was on a thin walkway at the very top of the flies. It was dizzying. I heard a piano. It was the New York City Ballet Company during an actual performance, and I had a Busby Berkeley view of it. I would visit this spot often during the next few weeks. It was better to be at this height, looking down at a corps de ballet, than to be dangling from the rafters of a 19th Century opera house in Kingston, Jamaica.

The corps de ballet for *Brigadoon* was under the direction of James "Jamie" Jamieson. He was a spry seventy years-old and had been mounting productions of *Brigadoon* since he helped create the original one in 1947. His body was lean and looked more like that of a man of twenty. He was all over the room, correcting postures, making adjustments, and moving the arms and limbs of the dancers into the correct silhouettes. They were like pieces of furniture for him. He had the energy and freshness of a new camper and was fully animated. He actually had Scottish roots and wore a kilt to the opening night performance. He reminded me of a character from *The Red Shoes*.

The dancers in *Brigadoon* were young; their average age was about twenty-two. This was a bit different from the seasoned "line," as it's called on Broadway, of somewhat older, slightly cynical types who are often called "gypsies." This term refers to their somewhat nomadic existence, which leads them to be where the job is at any particular time and determines their roots (or lack thereof), as long as they are active in the business.

Broadway gypsies wear a thick skin most of the time and have come to suspect that the worst is ahead of them at any given moment. They are always underpaid, always the least-appreciated for their discipline and hard work, and prone to injuries. The dancers I saw at the State Theatre radiated enthusiasm and innocence. They had some of the few steady jobs dancers could have. They performed in several productions each year from season to season, and were assured of at least six or seven months of salary. That's what made this experience different from the usual "commercial" roll of the dice. This was a permanent family, an institution, and it felt relatively stable.

No actor of my acquaintance has ever entered his dressing room to find a bottle of make-up remover and ample amounts of Kleenex waiting for him. There's always a mirror, a table, a wash basin, hooks, hangers, and even one's name on the door, but free Kleenex was a first in my experience. It seemed they were going to *make me up*! One hour prior to each performance, I sat in the make-up chair and for twenty minutes, I was lined, shadowed, highlighted, and color corrected by a man named Robert Baker. His job carried the same hazards as a good bartender's. He hears everything, whether he wants to or not. He sees the real nerves and insecurities, the sub-life of everyone who passes through his chair. He is almost like a Father Confessor. When he was finished with me I looked like Laurence Olivier as Oedipus. I hated to take it off after the show. It was a little too much for the street, though, even if it was the West Side.

On opening night after "places" had been called, I sat center-stage on a piece of scenery shaped like a boulder and waited for the show to begin. I could hear the muffled hubbub of the audience through the fabric of the heavy, red velvet curtain in front of me. Finally, the lights in the huge auditorium dimmed out, the audience settled down, and the curtain went up. A foot in front of me was a black-netted wall of scrim. There was also a scrim upstage masking the chorus, which began to sing the opening notes of *Brigadoon.* In a moment, the lights onstage would gradually bump up and I would become visible to the house for the first time.

Suddenly, my ankles felt wet. I looked down and I was standing in a cloud. The cloud was made from dry ice and spewed from the wings by huge ducts resembling Terry Gilliam's sewage pipes from *Brazil.* I thought, "I can't believe I'm getting paid to do this."

It was the easiest stage world I've ever had to believe in. What's more, I was playing a character who didn't believe in it!

At the bows, I looked up to see the spotlights criss-crossing the vast audience until they rested on three boxes in the first ring. There, in the little pinpoint of white light, waving to the audience below was Agnes DeMille, the original choreographer, sitting next to Frederick Loewe, the composer, and Lawrence Wien, the financier who had made it all possible. I was glad I had taken the job. How lucky can you get?

A Christmas Carol

My sister and I observed few rituals growing up, but we never missed the annual broadcast of *A Christmas Carol* starring Alastair Sim. We would push or drag a pair of giant upholstered armchairs to within a few feet of our twelve-inch television screen and settle in to enjoy two hours of mesmerizing drama interrupted only by commercials, during which we raided the icebox.

Sim was playing in a theatre not far from mine while I was in *Promises, Promises* in London. We met at some West End event and exchanged pleasantries. Our weekly schedules were identical, so it prevented either of us from seeing the other's performance. This was a real disappointment for me, and he politely expressed a similar regret. It was a big deal for me to meet him because I considered him to be one of the finest actors in the world. It didn't matter how many times I watched Mr. Sim's Scrooge, I always found something new about his performance to make me chuckle.

Thirty years later, I naturally jumped at the offer to play Scrooge at Madison Square Garden. It was a tough gig. There were fifteen shows a week for six weeks, and many of them started at nine o'clock in the morning. This is almost twice the number of performances given by a Broadway show each week. By the third show of the day, it became difficult to remember which one I was in the middle of.

During the finale, I had to run from the far left side of the audience all the way to the far right aisle while distributing candy to a multitude of outstretched hands. This seemed like a fun idea until I discovered that the width of the theatre was approximately an entire city block long. I was weighted down by under-dressing, and my progress was often impeded by children wandering into the aisle. I had to step back up onto the stage at a set point in the music and then sing the ten-minute finale "full-out," as they say, with Tiny Tim on my shoulder. I was blessed that my lungs were working at all by that time, breathing the dense and noxious white smoke used to produce a myriad of special effects in the show. It was sometimes impossible to see two feet in front of my face. It took its toll on the singers too, who rotated in and out of the show nursing various bronchial ailments.

As you know by now, I have never liked being up in high places (aside from the flies of the State Theatre). I don't suffer from vertigo, but ever since a boyhood pal (it was Marty Coppersmith, again) insisted that I join him on the roller coaster at Coney Island—it was that or be denied subway fare to get home, and I'd run out of money—I have had trouble keeping my knees from shaking whenever there's a chance I might fall ten feet to the floor.

In *How Now, Dow Jones* I was tossed in the air at the end of my big number eight times a week and caught horizontally by three chorus boys. I did everything I could to be nice to these fellas I was landing on, and they were absolute pros, but I can't say I ever enjoyed it.

At Madison Square Garden, I wore a leather harness under my costume so that, unseen by the audience, wire cables could be attached to it and lift me up in the air to dangle above one thousand squealing preteens. I was promised I would only be suspended for a few moments, then be lowered gently down to the deck. Of course, during one show, there was a glitch in the computer which controlled all this, and I hung up there for what seemed an eternity. I felt like a yo-yo on a string. I didn't want the kids to think I was afraid, so I had to pretend that I was supposed to be dangling around that way. It felt like camp all over again, making sure my audience laughed with me, never at me.

The entire ordeal was worth it, just to speak the lines I knew so well. *A Christmas Carol* is the quintessential story of spiritual transformation. Scrooge is man at his worst, then at his best. The production was ambitious, with detailed sets that recreated a period London cityscape. There was a huge cast, the music and choreography were first-rate, and best of all, the company became a family. During the holidays, that's all one could wish for. There was little turnover from one year to the next, and the cast bonded as they shared December's rituals with each other. I've always thought that the backstage world was a microcosm of the world at its best. All those different skills, practiced by an army of disparate individuals with little in common beyond their shared love and respect for make-believe.

There were children everywhere. Children in the show itself, brothers and sisters of company members brought from home to hang around in the wings, not to mention the hundreds of children who screeched with glee during the ominous opening chords of the overture.

I have never been a morning person, but as I stood in the dark, waiting to make my first entrance, the high-pitched peals of joy I heard got my blood pumping every time.

As providence would have it, in 2013 I was cast as Scrooge in the New York Public Radio production of *A Christmas Carol,* broadcast nationwide during the week of Christmas. This time, I stood in front of a microphone surrounded by the regulars on the station staff. They played all the other characters, switching roles with ease, and the whole event was over in a day. I still found the story easy to believe in, on every level, and this time I didn't have to worry about heights and cables. This time, all I had to worry about was sounding too much like Alastair Sim. I tasked myself to become my own curmudgeon, but certain performances are too iconic to ever erase. For me, his will always be one of them.

Long Runs

Many fine professional actors have never known what it's like to be in a long run. Only a relative handful of performers get to do that. By a long run, I mean at *least* six months.

On Broadway, the average show is at its best about six weeks after it has opened. Only then do the actors really own the material. By that, I mean that they can make it work consistently, eight times a week. By then, the material has been broken down into its smallest components and the best way to perform it has been found. But six weeks is only the very beginning of a long run. Six months later, it will require a lot of effort to keep it fresh.

Civilians often ask how actors can repeat their performances night after night. As a matter of fact, this question is second in frequency only to "How in the world did you memorize all those lines?" Although most audiences won't see any differences in a performance from night to night, the actor himself may experience a wide variety of emotions during his performance. Zero Mostel once said that after he was in a show for a while his performance energy on a particular night was affected by the kind of day he may have had.

It takes discipline to survive a long run. It means planning the entire day so that one is at the peak of one's creative enthusiasm at curtain time. Meals, exercise, sleep, social engagements, all have to adjust to the eight-performance schedule. If an actor is weak from dieting or too much exercise, it will show up in the performance. It might not be noticeable to someone seeing the play for the first time, but it would be noticeable to the director or producer, should they happen to be in the house. A good stage manager will go out front at least once a week and take notes. Actors are grateful for this input because, without a third eye, it's impossible to see what changes accumulate over time. The changes may be so subtle that it can take two months for a two-beat pause to grow into a four-beat pause, but the two-beat pause was the way it worked. It's difficult to stay on top of this without outside help. When George Abbott revisited his production of *Take Her, She's Mine* on Broadway, he posted a notice to the cast that read:

> There will be a rehearsal tomorrow,
> the purpose of which will be to
> take out all the "improvements."

What he really meant was schtick.

Even the Lunts could lose their laughs and not know why. In a famous example, Sir Alfred was helpless to explain why he had lost his laugh after the line, "May I have a cup o' tea, please?" The joke was that his appearance spoke of a man more likely to ask for a shot of whiskey but, after getting a consistent response to the line for weeks, somehow it had lost its ability to provoke a laugh. "What am I doing wrong?" he asked his brilliant partner Lynn Fontanne.

"You got the laugh in the first place because you were asking for a cup of tea. Now you're asking for a laugh. Ask for the tea and you'll find the laugh again." The sound of laughter is a surprise to an actor the first time he hears it, but once having done so he has lost his virginity. Most lost laughs can be attributed to this subtle change in awareness. If you expect the laugh, you won't get it. Don't expect it, and you will. As Carol Channing once observed, "As soon as an actor becomes aware of a quality in his personality — it's gone!" Human nature being what it is, few actors are ready to admit that a lost laugh is their own fault. There are always excuses. Most common among these is that the laugh was lost because someone in the audience coughed on the operative word of the setup or punch line of a particular joke. Or, there was no laugh because the setup wasn't clearly spoken, which means the culprit may be the other actor.

Boredom is inevitable. Kurt Kazner, veteran of stage and screen, had been in *Barefoot in the Park* since it opened, and when his vacation loomed, his attention would wander off before he physically left. Once, in anticipation of his freedom, he left the theatre after the second act and headed for the bus stop on Eighth Avenue. He forgot that

Barefoot in the Park had three acts and that his character had to make an important entrance in Act III. Fortunately, the stage manager got to him before the bus did, and the audience was spared the confusion of seeing an entirely new actor when the understudy came on as his character. Another time, he fell asleep in the dressing room and, when his cue came, the stage manager, not seeing him in his usual place, began to call his name over the backstage squawk box. Unfortunately, the name "Kurt," through the speakers, sounded like "Curtain" to the crew, who were playing poker in the basement. They ran to their posts and, to everyone's astonishment, lowered the curtain. At this point, the act was only ten minutes old, so the audience knew something had gone wrong. An announcement was made, and we started again from the top.

I've been guilty of some long-run-induced antics myself. I once tried to get the gentle-spoken Kay Medford, another seasoned veteran, to break character during the run of *Don't Drink The Water* by delivering a line to her from a closer than normal proximity. She very politely took a hold of my arm and, without missing a beat, walked me right into the wings and offstage. She managed this while remaining on stage herself, and it was up to me to re-enter after having been completely erased as it were, as well as humiliated. I never tried it again.

Late in the run of *How Now, Dow Jones*, our audiences began to dwindle. Playing to small audiences can be demoralizing, so we decided to elect a Morale Officer of the Day to divert our spirits and lighten our hearts. There were 40 people in the cast, and each day a different person filled the role. We had bake-offs, swap-meets and casinos in the basement of the theater. We entertained ourselves at intermission in the green room with original mini-musicals or parodies of our own performances. Someone even made a piñata! My idea was to have a scavenger hunt. I cut up two-dozen small pieces of red paper and hid them all over the backstage areas. I even went further and hid them on the set as well. The person to collect the most pieces of paper would be the winner. As a result, at any given moment, the audience might see a member of the company directing his gaze around the stage as if he'd lost something. Thanks to the common sense of the stage managers, this game was short-lived.

In *Doubles*, a story about four friends who meet once a week to play tennis, I was directed to weigh myself on the locker room scale several times during the play. I was playing a hypochondriac who was, naturally, obsessed with his health. The audience always laughed as I stepped up on the scale, and the laugh would grow as I fiddled with the small metal weights on the bar in front of me. I thought they were laughing because I was weighing myself with such serious purpose. But the laughter was prompted by a piece of stage business invented by my co-star, the Tony Award-winner for *Angels in America*, Ron Liebman. Unbeknownst to me, each time I got on the scale, he pressed his foot on it behind my back. The audience loved it. Liebman loved it. I was the only one in the theater who didn't know about it until after the show closed, which was too late for proportionate revenge.

Sometimes even the crew can get involved in a prank. During the run of *Barefoot in the Park*, the leading lady, Penny Fuller, was visited by her mother from North Carolina. It was Penny's birthday, and she knew her mother was in the theater, presumably in the audience, but never expected to hear her voice through the earpiece of the onstage phone during a performance. The electrician had managed this feat and it gave Penny a shock, along with a weird sense of displacement as her mother wished her a happy birthday from a backstage sound booth.

The most daring practical joke I ever saw was initiated by, perhaps the most admired and loved actor-dancer on Broadway, Scott Wise. We were roommates during the run of *Jerome Robbins' Broadway* in New York, Los Angeles, and Tokyo. Scott adhered to the tradition that "anything goes on closing night." In fact, this "tradition" can encourage excessively mischievous pranks.

On the last night of the run in New York, Mr. Wise carried a concealed "Whoopee Cushion" on stage with him during one of the early song-and-dance numbers. The scene involved three couples sitting around a table at a nightclub. They were there to cheer up one of their friends who was depressed. During the number, each of them sang and danced their particular solos, and then returned to their seats.

At a prescribed moment, when the choreography allowed it, Scott produced the "Whoopee Cushion" from under his costume and in one fell swoop, placed it onto the empty chair next to him. Then he watched as the actress finished her verse and sat down hard on an accented note in the orchestral arrangement. Her face registered horror as the prolonged exhalation of air greeted her, with its twisted, awful sound. She knew instantly it was Scott's joke, and was unable to utter any sound at all for the rest of the scene.

The entire company stood in the wings watching the events unfold. Her face went bright red, partly from embarrassment but mostly because of the enormous effort it took to suppress laughter. As with most pranks when they come off as well as this one did, there is a chain reaction that affects the perpetrators. None of the performers on stage in that number could sing the end of the song.

Mildred Natwick, who appeared in many John Ford films, was in *Barefoot in the Park*, and had her own way of dealing with the daily grind. One of the hard facts of life about a long run is that it's possible to face a full house on a Saturday night, but only a third of a house at the beginning of the week. The laughs will still come in all the same places, but they will be briefer and harder to hear. This can feel like telling a joke to an empty room. Millie couldn't resist the temptation to comment on this paradox, and did so under her breath in a sing-song commentary heard by the other actors, but never the audience. A line which rocked the rafters the night before might produce no reaction at all, and the little melody she sang to herself would be sung in a minor key. At other times, she produced a light, trilling sound when she felt heartened by a particularly good response. She got every laugh there was, and kept the rest of the cast well-entertained.

Then there is the matter of understudies. When one of them goes on for the first time, the entire company buzzes with anticipation. Everyone sends their positive energy to the neophyte both on and off stage. While in front of the audience, the cast will rivet their attention on this new presence in their midst and shape their performance to fit what suits the moment. This intuitive generosity explains why almost nobody gives a bad first performance. The play will be conformed to fill in the blanks in the understudy's performance wherever they may be. By the second or third time, the regulars will reclaim their territory and the newcomer will be judged in a harsher light.

Sometimes a change of cast can improve things. The lines will be heard "fresh" by the players, as if for the first time, and the cast will adjust to accommodate a new presence. But the biggest challenge of a long run is to keep your own performance alive and interesting to yourself. A good deal of acting is the ability to fool yourself. During the rehearsal period, the actor selects the images he needs in order to do that but, as he uses them over and over, the images will lose their effect and need to be replaced. Good actors feel this happening to them and feed themselves new images on the spot. I've found it's helpful to spend some time during the day imagining something new about the character so you can play with renewed enthusiasm if not innocence.

Long runs provide a rare period of stability and normalcy in an actor's life. It's the only time he ever settles into a routine or is able to plan a vacation. Unfortunately, most of his life may feel like a vacation, but not one he can afford.

My mother had an uncanny ability to predict things. She announced one day, after seeing the movie *Victor/Victoria*, that I would be well-cast in the role played by Robert Preston if it were made into a Broadway musical, which is exactly what happened fifteen years later. Blake Edwards had the same thought after I did a small role in a film he made called *Switch* starring Ellen Barkin. I even played a small role in a television movie starring his wife, Julie Andrews.

Playing the role of Toddy for two years opposite Julie Andrews was to experience real class. There is no more disciplined a professional that I can name, nor a kinder one. She became an example to us all of what it means to exhibit grace under pressure, and there was a great deal of pressure for several reasons. The rehearsal period was lengthy, the pre-Broadway tryout extensive, the sets and costumes expensive, and the expectations for it to be a winner were tremendous. Along with these elements was also the unfortunate truth that Blake, for all his contributions to film, comedy, and drama, had never directed a Broadway musical. He definitely learned how, but while he did, there were a few bumps along the way. He also allowed the press to eavesdrop on the progress of the show before it was ready to be sold. The critics, who always feel that an end run is being attempted when this is done in order to dampen their impact, are always quick to punish such a tactic, and they did with *Victor/Victoria.* Through it all, "Jooles," as Dame Julie Andrews is known by all who love her, was a mixture of Mary Poppins and the Queen of England. There's true royalty in her blood.

Former President Gerald Ford and Henry Kissinger were in my dressing room on the opening night of *Victor/Victoria* because there was no longer room for them across the hall in Julie Andrews' room. Mrs. Ford wasn't there because she was at her clinic in California at the time. Her husband offered his chair to my father who was, needless to say, surprised to see him. (I confess to being very peeved at President Ford when he granted a pardon to Richard Nixon after the Watergate debacle, but he was so affable that I could bear him no malice. We had met years earlier when he and the first lady came backstage to visit Lucie Arnaz and me after a performance of *They're Playing Our Song.*)

He liked *Victor/Victoria* and told me that he would come and see it again with his wife. Several months later they both appeared at my dressing room door.

"You see, Tony," he said. "I kept my word and came back!"

"I'll never doubt you again, Mr. President." I replied.

"Then you're the only one." he said.

One of the finer aspects of being in a long run, in addition to being able to pay your rent, is the sense of family which comes from spending so much time together. Eight shows a week assures that you will celebrate birthdays and holidays with the company, and Sunday brunches in the basement before the last matinee of the week. Some crews set up elaborate barbecue apparatus in the alley next to their stage door and feed the entire cast.

I was starring with Linda Lavin and Michele Lee in Charles Busch's *The Tale of the Allergist's Wife* at the Barrymore Theatre on that fateful day in September, 2001. Broadway came to a standstill. The first three performances of the week were cancelled throughout the neighborhood. In addition to absorbing the scope of what had happened and feeling a new vulnerability previously unimagined, it also felt unnatural to be separated from one's coworkers during this tragedy. When we returned to work on Thursday night, usually the fourth show of the week, we greeted each other with swollen eyes and deep hugs. We were a family, again, and there was great comfort in that. We also felt lucky to be alive.

It was no surprise that the size of our audiences shrank from what we were used to. In fact, there were less than two hundred people per performance during the first two weeks after 9/11, down from over a thousand. We didn't mind. We just cared about giving the best show to those who showed up. We were living with a heightened sense of our own mortality, and were grateful for the sense of normalcy the show provided. In the vast emptiness of Times Square at that time, the theatre really did become a haven for us, like a little ship in a storm-tossed sea. An eerie quiet permeated the theatre district for several months. After all, Times Square was a logical target if the terrorists sought to destroy the city's commercial viability. There was the Anthrax scare, soon after. No one knew what would happen next, and people were afraid. When we mingled in the basement of our own theatre, it made us think of London during the Blitz. There was even a decision by the producers to alter the text of the play because it included the word "terrorist." They felt that it might distance the audience from the comedy they were supposed to be enjoying.

As terrifying an event as 9/11 was for anyone living in New York City, it deeply affected Americans across the country in ways that would soon be made clear to those of us who worked on Broadway.

Alvina Krause would be proven right. What she had predicted forty years ago would now be played out in front of our theatre. Large groups of average-looking people would assemble in the street every night, resembling a crowd of extras from a Frank Capra movie. They stood in the cold and the rain wanting to say, "Thank you." to the cast they had just been entertained by. These were not regular theatregoers at all. Many had never been to New York City before. They organized themselves in places like Concord, Massachusetts and Erie, Pennsylvania. There was very little air travel going on, so they came in chartered buses at their own expense, answering the pleas of Mayor Giuliani to support the City of New York.

I believe there was a more primal reason for their pilgrimage, a reason Alvina Krause had preached about all her life. She believed in the sacred, transforming power of live theatre. She knew that in a time of crisis, people would want to be together and that the theatre would give them a sense of connection with the rest of humanity. These Grant Wood types and George Baileys from around America sensed that and, for a short time, West 47th Street was more like Bedford Falls in *It's a Wonderful Life* than the usual traffic zone for pickpockets and panhandlers.

In keeping with the somber mood of the times, it was fitting that my next challenge would be a weighty one. I was offered the role of Hamm in Samuel Beckett's *Endgame* by the Irish Repertory Company. When I was a freshman acting student at Northwestern, the theatre department was putting on a production of Beckett's *Waiting for Godot.* I was assigned to write a paper about it and found it hard to make sense of, but it was compelling and it made me think. *Endgame*, written years later, was the last act of it. For years I'd longed for the chance to sink my teeth into a play of substance, and here it was.

Hamm is described as being blind but wearing dark glasses, according to the author's stage directions. I decided in the name of "artistic integrity" to keep my eyes shut during the entire ninety minutes it took to perform. The audience would have no way of knowing whether my eyes were open or not, but I wanted to see if the reality of blindness provided any deeper insight into the role. It made it easier to connect to much that seemed obscure in the play because I could live entirely in my imagination, which I discovered is heightened when deprived of visual input. I also learned that with my eyes shut, the musculature of my face felt different, but in a good way. It was unlike anything I'd ever experienced. After seeing a performance of it, my own daughter admitted that she didn't know who I was up there. I'm not sure I did either. I was exhilarated by it at first because it was liberating. When I opened my eyes at the curtain call, I felt as if I'd just awakened from a dream, but I'd been in a tunnel for an hour and a half and found it increasingly lonely and isolating. It didn't help that the subject matter of *Endgame* is unrelentingly bleak and depressing.

We were booked for eight weeks and as we neared the end of the run I began to dread going into that tunnel every night. I missed making eye contact with my fellow actors. I missed the connection. Anyone familiar with *Endgame* knows that it consists of repeated rituals and line patterns interspersed with abstract stories that reflect life's deepest mysteries.

There is one particular bit of dialogue that is repeated no less than nine times. Each time, the subsequent plot, such as it exists, moves forward in a different way. I had a list on my dressing room mirror of the nine variations with catchwords alongside so I could remember them. I should have taken the list onstage with me because during one of the previews, with critics in the house, I skipped the fourth variation and, by so doing, cut out six pages of text which the audience would never hear. I also stymied my costar, who realized what I had done long before I ever became aware of it. He also knew that the cut I'd made meant that several props, necessary to make sense of the events in the play, would never make their way onto the stage.

Adam Heller, playing Clov, the faithful servant—son, slave, whatever—arrived at a show-saving solution. He went offstage, while speaking his lines, and reentered carrying every prop the play required from that moment onward. Of course, as my eyes were closed, I hadn't a clue as to what he was doing, and couldn't make sense of the noise near my feet (I was in a wheelchair) as he dropped several items on the floor, which we would need as we went on.

As we filed down the narrow stairway to our dressing rooms afterwards, I asked what all the commotion had been about. It was the first moment I became aware of what I had done. Thank heaven *Endgame* is obscure and, to the best of my knowledge, none of the aisle-sitters present ever mentioned the omission in their reviews. Maybe sometimes it's true that "less is more."

As luck would have it, I was destined to go from one extreme to another. My next opportunity was so extreme, in fact, that I initially returned the script to my agent and said, in effect, "No way!" As much as I thought Beckett's *Endgame* bizarre, I thought Beane's *Xanadu* was off the charts!

I didn't "get it" then, and I don't think I "got it" on closing night. More power to the producers, and particularly to Douglas Carter

Beane, who persisted until I agreed to take part in a workshop production somewhere in Greenwich Village. As it turned out, it pleased the invited audience, and several months later we were in rehearsal for a Broadway run. I was convinced this would be the worst debacle of my career, but, once again, I got lucky. The Times loved it and so did most of the opinion-makers. On opening night, Joan Rivers was the first person to come backstage, and she had only one complaint: she wanted me to be on roller skates at the curtain call. I told her it was a fun idea, but I had specified in my contract that under no circumstances could I be prevailed upon to wear roller skates. I couldn't stand them as a kid, and I wasn't going to end up with broken bones, just for a few laughs. I was smart because a week before the critics came, the leading actor fell off his skates while demonstrating a simple swivel and missed the entire run. He was replaced by Cheyenne Jackson, and the rest is history.

The Accident

January 20, 2009

I performed in *Xanadu* for a year without missing a single show. No roller skates, no injuries. In 2009, two months after the show closed on Broadway, I happened to slip on a small area rug in my bathroom (how humiliating after having survived so many close calls!) and knocked my head on something hard as I fell. That's the last thing I remember about the entire incident. I was alone in my apartment at the time and was discovered, unconscious, five hours later, by my daughter. She had been alerted that I hadn't shown up for a luncheon. I also wasn't answering my phone. I was rushed to the hospital and kept in an induced coma for seven days. When I woke up, I discovered that I could no longer speak English, write words, or recognize any of the names in my address book. The doctors told me I had suffered an acute subdural hematoma; bleeding between the brain and the skull. The same thing had happened to the actress Natasha Richardson, but she was far from a proper facility and died shortly after a brief recovery. I *did* recover, thanks to modern medicine and the efforts by my daughter to ensure that I had the best care. Oddly enough, I was in the same hospital where I was born almost seventy years earlier.

"Where am I?" I asked.

"You're in Lenox Hill Hospital." my daughter assured me. "You've been here for almost a week. They've kept you in an induced coma because they weren't sure how you might react when you woke up. The doctors say it's a miracle you're alive."

"How did I get here, anyway? I can't seem to remember what happened to me. I don't think I was sick." In fact, I was healthy, reasonably fit, and prided myself for having missed fewer performances during a five-decade career than most of my peers. I'd been recently examined by my internist, dentist, ophthalmologist, and so forth. So, why in the hell was I here? Was that a door off in the distance? Someone was leaning over me. I went back to sleep.

So it was for several weeks. In time, the door became more outlined but I had an existential problem. How did I get here, and what to do now? I first wondered about such things in my crib. I had the same cautiously optimistic expectations then as now, as I gradually awoke from an extended coma. I felt confused, but privileged. Whatever happened to me, I was in a comfortable bed and being attended to. I was here, but where?

I didn't know if I had suffered any permanent damage to my memory banks as a result of the fall. People over sixty have trouble remembering a lot of things, but it's impossible to know what you don't know. I felt like an archivist of my own past. I could remember places, people, and events from decades ago easily, but there were blank spaces where memories of the four weeks before the surgery should be. The brain itself, according to the experts, did not fully deposit the information into the hard drive. It was never recorded, so it can't be replayed. The same thing happened in my post-operative state. The brain wasn't able to record for a while then, either. For those eight weeks I could have been Rip Van Winkle. I do remember wanting to escape from the hospital while experiencing what they call "steroid rage." I wouldn't believe the story they were telling me. They said I had been operated on and that I was not permitted to leave the room, let alone the hospital. There was a male orderly sitting next to the bed and I thought I recognized him as a bouncer from Elaine's. I told them they were trying to kidnap me, or had mistaken me for someone else because I happened to be a famous person. They looked at me as though I was nuts. I also told them that I wasn't fooled by all the newspapers I couldn't read. They were in a foreign language in an attempt to confuse me. At one point I told the orderly I was leaving at sun-up. I put on my street clothes and sat on the edge of the bed, waiting for dawn so I would be able to find my way home once I hit the streets. When the early morning light streamed through the window, I rose to my feet and stood nose to nose with the orderly, who had risen with me. I realized I wasn't going anywhere.

A week later, I persuaded a nurse to purchase a copy of a local newspaper, which I insisted be bought from someplace several blocks from the hospital. I saw myself at the center of a vast conspiracy. Talk about wacko. I even scared myself in the mirror because they had only shaved my head where they needed to in order to remove my scalp. I looked like the crazy guy in *One Flew Over the Cookoo's Nest*, or the crazy guy in *Fargo* who funneled his friend into the wood chopper. I was scaring the other patients. My first big step in recovery was to get a haircut!

Was this it for me? Did the whole world know about it? Was my career over? Only time would tell, but so far my "incident" had been kept out of the newspapers. An actor only makes the front page if he falls down during a show in front of an audience, and that wouldn't happen until a few months later.

What a perfect story to add to my memoir, I thought. I'd been working on a memoir for about a decade. It's every actor's dream to write a memoir and have it published, but it's tough to produce one if you've lost your memory. How was *that* going to work out? What I really needed was a plot. Where would my story begin? Even trickier, how would it end? This was all becoming very existential.

My daughter brought me back to my apartment. I had suffered three broken ribs, a deflated lung, a broken collar bone, and forty-two days of hospital food. I was finally thinner than I ever wanted to be.

I accepted a few offers for small gigs as I tip-toed back into my career. I appeared in a short satiric revue at Symphony Space, a large auditorium on the Upper West Side. I even shared a bill with my old friend from Northwestern, Richard Benjamin. We did a reading of Neil Simon's *The Sunshine Boys* at a benefit to raise money for a theatre company based in New Jersey.

I did a job on *Law & Order*, and a one-night cabaret act at The O'Neill Center in Connecticut with Penny Fuller. We performed an hour's worth of songs and patter, some sad, some funny, and did it in front of about 200 people. It went well, but I felt relieved when it was over. I didn't know what to expect out there under the bright lights. There were a few awkward pauses as I remember, but I also recall being able to ad-lib my way through them without embarrassment. I was "riding on velvet," an old vaudeville term to describe what heaven it is to condition an audience to your rhythm so that they laugh whether you say something funny or not.

At any rate, I was glad to feel I was up to the next challenge, whatever that might be. It came in the form of an offer from the Manhattan Theatre Club to play the producer in a revival of *The Royal Family*, a role played by my first Broadway mentor, Sam Levene, in the first revival of the play forty years earlier. I wanted to be at the top of my game. I wanted to know my lines early, remember my blocking from the previous rehearsal, and construct a series of beats, or landings, for myself so I could feel free to express my inner life, or subtext, within the space and time allotted by the director. This was an ensemble piece so there were a lot of stories that needed to be told. The process gets easier the quicker you own your lines, or are "off-book." Julie Andrews once assured me during the out-of-town tryout for *Victor/Victoria* that the "Line Fairy," as she referred to it, would never desert me. The fairy would land in the middle of my forehead at exactly the moment I was supposed to say my line.

For the first time in my life I couldn't remember them with confidence, even after the third week of rehearsal. I was having trouble and keeping everybody waiting. No one ever registered anything but understanding and sympathy, but I think they believed it was my age that was the cause of the problem. It wasn't. It was the effect of my operation and the length of time it takes for the brain to heal. They didn't know about that and forgave me for being slow, just as I had done with elderly actors I had worked with over the years, but I never dreamed that would happen to me.

The first few performances went smoothly, but on my first afternoon matinee since my recovery from surgery eight months earlier, something didn't feel right. I couldn't be sure what it was but as I went through my usual routine, collecting my hat and cane from the prop table offstage right, saying soft "hello's" to the wardrobe people huddled in the wings, and taking a few deep breaths, something felt different. I thought about my "super objective" and my purpose for visiting the family at this juncture and what I hoped to accomplish before I left, but I still couldn't think of my first line. Not to worry, Julie Andrews told me the line would be there in my head when I needed it. I climbed the three steps to the platform I was meant to be on and waited for my cue to enter.

This was the fourth play I had done for Manhattan Theatre Club, so I may have received some small entrance applause, I don't remember. I still hadn't heard the line in my head, but was surprised to discover that I was speaking anyway. I could tell from the sound of my voice in my ears. There was a solid laugh from the audience that had never been there before. It was unexpected and unintended. Rosemary Harris, a great actress and a dear lady, turned her head in my direction and gave me a querulous look. It seemed to say, "Has there been a rehearsal that I was not aware of? Are you saying the lines as written, or are you adding something else?"

As it turns out, there was a similar guffaw at the end of each of my lines. I was speaking a language very close to Polish. I don't speak Polish, and I was certainly not supposed to be speaking it in this play in front of all these people. Then, the reliable Jan Maxwell, as yet to make her first entrance, was suddenly walking towards me, hand extended, and led me gently to the chaise at stage center. She asked me first to sit down and then to lie on the floor. I did as I was told feeling like a little boy being led somewhere by his mother. I watched the stage curtain descend within the proscenium and fall to the floor, just as it had in *Citizen Kane* and *Singin' in the Rain,* and that's the last thing I remember.

I woke up a few hours later in St. Luke's Hospital in the care of a neurologist who explained what had happened to me. It was the doctor's belief that I had suffered a seizure. That's what he diagnosed when I was "delivered" to him. Seizures can be prevented with certain medicines, which I had been prescribed when I left the care of my previous hospital administrators, but at some point I was granted permission to discontinue the dosage because I complained that it was making me tired. Like many others, I couldn't accept the idea that I wasn't fully recovered when I clearly was not.

The next day, the story was on the front page of The New York Times. What a bummer! My previous mishap at home put me out of commission for six months, and I had been able to keep news of it from ever getting out, but if you shutter a packed Broadway theatre on a Sunday matinee, it gets around. It wasn't as if I'd died, although it's unlikely the audience had ever seen anything like it before. They were given refunds and sent home early. "Is this the end of Little Ricco?" asks Edward G. Robinson, the quintessential tough guy with a heart of gold, as he lies in the gutter at the end of *Little Caesar*, his body riddled with bullet holes. I was asking myself the same question.

After a night in the hospital and two days off, I showed up at the theatre for opening night. My daughter thought I was crazy, but I felt perfectly up for it. I convinced everyone at the theatre that I could handle it, but they wisely urged me to make use of something known in the business as the "plug." It's a tiny speaker that fits in your ear and allows you to be fed a line you might not remember from a stage manager's assistant, who is seated in a small booth at the rear of the balcony. He sat in front of a microphone with a script in his hand. If I forgot a line his voice was right there in my ear to prompt me along. Strange as it seemed to me and my daughter, I didn't need it. I was functioning from remembered behavior.

I played the entire eight-week run, but never attempted a two-show day. My understudy did the matinees. There were times when I was grateful to have the plug. It put my mind at ease to know it was there. It also taught me something I had never thought about before. When an actor speaks a line, he knows what he's going to say before it comes out of his mouth, but when he speaks it because he hears it in his ear, his behavior will be more in sync with the way people act in real life. We all speak before we think most of the time, and adjust our behavior to the way we sound. It permits you to feel more as if you're in the moment. I think that's why Marlon Brando chose later in his career to use the device, and others as well. It forces you to mean what you say just like a real person does without the extra layer of "here is how I'm going to say it" getting in the way.

Six years later, fans and acquaintances will still stop me in the street to ask, with consoling concern, if I'm alright. I know they mean well, but I'm surprised because that "slip on the ice," as I view it, happened a long time ago.

The final verdict is still out on the long range impact of my swan dive at the Milton J. Friedman theatre on 47th Street, in the heart of Times Square. It was the same theatre where I spent eighteen-months in *Barefoot in the Park* when I was twenty-five years-old.

Restarting my career after the accident was like remembering who I used to be, and how much I missed the habit of going to work, and all that comes with it. *That's* a familiar role. *That's* how I know myself.

At this juncture in my narrative, I feel compelled to assure the reader, if he's still here, that I am not intent on retelling the story of Job. It may seem so because the recent events in this narrative have dealt with a series of setbacks which may seem to parallel the bad fortunes of that biblical icon. I have revealed my financial undoing, the dangers of special effects film making, a double hernia operation, a mishap that resulted in life-threatening brain surgery, and the disruption of normalcy caused by the attack on the World Trade Center. These incidents were, to say the least, downers, but I perceived them at the time, and in retrospect, as obstacles placed in the way of my evolution by the whims of fate. The pundits say: into each life a little rain must fall. From where I sit as I write this, I still see the glass half full rather than half empty. There have been too many blessings, too many happy coincidences and fortunate outcomes for me to imagine that any of the setbacks I endured were part of some curse designed by the furies to thwart my dreams and ambition. If anything, the opposite is closer to the truth. Based on the principle that we can never know what we don't know, it's impossible for me to be sure that I still have all the marbles I started with. It took months to recover my full sense of self and for at least the next two years I felt as if I was exiting a long tunnel. Gradually, I began to believe I could still remember lines and pick up a cue with my old confidence. I was a lucky son of a gun to have survived all of these temporal trials and tribulations. A happy ending is on the way. I promise.

Phase Five:
Who's Tony Roberts?

I was sitting on a bench in Central Park recently, not far from where I watched a military demonstration when I was a child. The bench is fondly referred to by those of us who sit on it regularly as "The Curmudgeon Bench." It observes the same lack of formality as a community beach in the summer. Folks may stay for five minutes or three hours, when the weather's nice. A few locals gather to discuss the headlines, observe the passing throng and the endless parade of dogs and strollers.

One late afternoon, as I was complaining to friends about something or other, a middle-aged woman suddenly stood before me with her arms folded and said, "I've seen you in something, but I can't place it. What have I seen you in?" I was having a hard time seeing her, as it happens, because the sun was setting behind her. All I could make out was a silhouette. I squinted up and replied, "I'll answer you as a friend of mine suggests, because he is often asked the same question. Why don't you tell me what you've seen and I'll tell you if I was in it."

I know this reply was a bit snarky, but so it goes sometimes on The Curmudgeon Bench. It's tough to explain why this question provokes such a dichotomy of reactions in me. On the one hand, I am delighted that someone, anyone really, knows I exist. On the downside, I am disappointed that her recollection is so incomplete. It even seems gutsy to me that a stranger would approach a person with no sense of shame about demanding to know who they are. She was not finished.

"Well, tell me one thing you did. Theatre, film, or TV."

Now I'm starting to bristle. "Okay. I've been in twenty-three Broadway shows, twenty-four films, and many TV shows. What do you see the most of?"

"TV," she says.

"Then it's probably an episode of *Law & Order*. They're on all the time." I did four episodes playing different roles many years ago, but they're all over the cable channels.

"That's it!" she says and turns away abruptly to join her friend waiting nearby. They're quickly off, in a cloud of dust.

This exchange leads to a discussion with a total stranger on the bench next to me who is startled that the woman who had just left never asked me my name. This was followed by a debate about the value of fame in general and what it was really worth. As an aspiring actress herself, and a very young one, she declared that she had no interest in becoming famous. She was more concerned with practicing the craft of acting. I admired her for her idealism, but had to throw in my own two cents.

"That's all well and good, but the very reason you walk on a stage, the thing that forces you to make an entrance, is the attention you seek. You want people to listen to you. Well… not *you*, but to the playwright. You need to be the focus of the room to do that. You need to say, 'Look at me! Look at me!' and that's because you either got too little attention as a child, or too much. Nobody knows." I don't think she expected such a florid reply. I couldn't stop. "And when it comes to making a living, obviously the people with 'names' make the most money over the course of their careers, but more significantly, they have the option to take the work that challenges and inspires them, and that enhances their reputations. There's also a case to be made that it's good to pay the rent."

My father would have been proud.

The ultimate paradox about fame is that it is the very thing that robs the actor of his most precious asset; his anonymity.

Johnny Carson once said to Robert Mitchum on *The Tonight Show*, "Why is it that whenever I see you in a movie you're always 'Robert Mitchum?'"

"Because that's who the audience came to see." he replied. "If the marquis says 'Robert Mitchum' then I have to show up, or they'll want their money back." He had a point.

Then there's a story about Sir Laurence Olivier who was being visited backstage by Spencer Tracy and Katherine Hepburn. He would spend two hours in front of the make-up mirror molding a character nose for

Richard III, whom he hoped to incarnate on a stage in London.

Spencer Tracy teased him by saying, "Tell me something, Larry. Who do you think they're going to think you are?"

It's a question that points to the vanity of all actors who presume to transform themselves into other people, but that's what drives us. Am I any of the characters I've played? Either all of them or none of them is the only answer.

Being recognized by strangers was not something that could be easily explained to my daughter when she was still at an age where I could carry her on my shoulders. We were wending our way through Midtown in this manner when occasionally some passerby would nod familiarly to me, or, in some cases say, "Hello, Tony." I always responded with what I thought was a humble and polite, "Thank you." and we would move on. At some point I had figured out that humility was the most appealing quality a human being could possess. As radio star Fred Allen said, "In Hollywood it's important to be sincere. If you can fake that—you've got it made."

Eventually, my daughter asked, "How come they all know you?" I had never considered how to explain such a phenomenon to a five-year-old.

After a brief pause, I said, "Well, they don't really know me, they just think they do because they've seen me on television, or in the movies, but they don't know me personally. They're not people I know back. They're not really friends of mine."

"Oh," she replied. A few moments later, when another stranger said he'd liked my work, she leaned into my ear and whispered, "You didn't really know him, did you?"

"That's right. How could you tell?"

"Your voice sounds different from the way you talk when it's someone you know."

She hit the nail on the head and was never confused again.

I realized at some point that it was necessary to adopt a different tone when dealing with fans than when speaking to people I had actually met previously. I never wanted to be rude to anybody, especially if they were paying me a compliment, so "meeting the fans" became like inhabiting a character of my own devising. The "switchover" served the need to behave graciously while simultaneously protecting my privacy. If my show of appreciation for the recognition didn't seem genuine and heartfelt to the stranger, then it would not be in my best interest. Fans generally don't like to be dismissed or unappreciated. So I would become this prefabricated "me" invested with enough conviction to keep the real "me" for my family, friends, and associates. Politicians do the same thing—Spencer Tracy once said he could have done worse in life than to become an actor. He could have been a politician! If you are doling yourself out to intimates and strangers in the same way, then any hint of credible sincerity will be hard to sustain in either circumstance.

This ability to create false identity, or to slip in and out of character is the thing that actors are trained to do, but I never thought that I would need to invent myself in the "real world" as anything other than who I felt like being at any particular moment. That doesn't always work out so well if someone stops at your table in a restaurant and waves a Playbill in your face as you're about to swallow a chicken bone. Or, as it happened to me on the opening night of a Broadway show, I was close enough to the autograph-seekers behind the barricades to overhear the following exchange, referring to me as I walked past:

"Is he anybody?"

"Nah, he's nobody."

As it turned out, these two guys were regulars at opening nights all over New York City. They may have even been brothers. I didn't appreciate the dismissal, but there was nothing I could do about it. It comes with the territory. It brought me great satisfaction a decade or so later when one of them pushed his way through a group of bystanders and asked for my autograph. Of course I recognized him. I smiled inside and out as I chose not to remind him of his prior evaluation of me.

Unlike most actors, I was usually employed in one way or another. My father's dictums resonated deeply; "Don't ever stop looking for the next job." he intoned. "This is a cruel and heartless business you've set your sights on, and you can never rest on your laurels. Make rounds, be on time, look like a professional, study your craft, take advantage of every opportunity, work begets work." His words became my mantra. I took his advice and it paid off, but also left me with a sense of insecurity. Regardless of how high I rose on the ladder of success, I never felt that I had "made it." Success is just a concept, not a place one can actually inhabit. Looking back I can see that I did "make it" and that it was all real, but at the time I felt I didn't exist without a contract in my hand. Right from the start, I had seen actors, myself included, fired and replaced during the first week of rehearsals, or because their parts were written out, or because they couldn't remember their lines, or just… because.

I mentioned earlier that my father had devoted a good many decades in the service of the unions he helped to establish. In 1988, he was given AFTRA's rarely bestowed George Heller Memorial Gold Card for his dedication to his fellow members. His devotion to that cause was not lost on me, and I was elected to serve on the Board of Directors of both Actors' Equity Association and The Screen Actors Guild. My father's advice to me about that was, "You'll be fine if you stick to your principles. Just try not to do anything divisive." Even now that seems contradictory, but he made it work. He was nicknamed "The Peacemaker." I met the best people in the business during my time on the boards. I had an easy time of it because, unlike my father, I wasn't forced to endure the devastating effect of the infamous "Blacklist" inflicted on the entertainment industry during the era of Senator Joseph McCarthy's reign of terror. Had it never happened, my father's career and those of many others at that time might have risen to a higher plane. As things played out, the fear spread by the House Un-American Activities Committee destroyed the lives of many innocent people. The forward momentum of my father's career was certainly affected. As a member of the board I was proud to participate in meetings long into the night debating the most seemingly insignificant details attached to resolutions that always appeared at first to be easily resolved, but rarely were. We were actors pretending to be lawyers, chasing the money our employers wanted to keep us from sharing. It was a privilege to serve.

April, 2012

In Central Park a man approaches me with a question. He's of medium height and looks like a taller Woody Allen. He introduces himself as the organizer of The Apocalyptic Film Festival that takes place annually in the city. I'm thinking this guy is a weirdo. "Are you the actor who wore the white garment with a green visor in *Annie Hall*?"

"Yes, that's me. Tony Roberts."

"How would you like to be on the panel of our forthcoming forum?" he inquires.

"No, thank you." I say, not wanting to witness an apocalypse before my time. He accepts my response cordially, and we each go our separate ways. Two weeks later, I was interviewed by Robert Osborne on the final night of the Turner Classic Movie Festival in Hollywood, where they were showing a newly restored print of *Annie Hall.* Why so much *Annie Hall* recognition all of a sudden, or so it seemed to me, and why was I being recognized so much lately? I thought I knew the answer; my haircut! For the last six months I was urged by a highly regarded hair stylist, whose prices were through the roof, to let my hair grow longer than it had ever been before. Unlike Max, I have a great head of hair. There, I said it! It looked okay, but when I looked in the mirror I didn't know who I was. It was my face framed in a bonnet. Finally, frustrated with all the attention it required to keep from looking like the neighborhood lunatic, I walked into an old-fashioned barber shop on Lexington Avenue and for thirty dollars got the same haircut I had in 1977 when *Annie Hall* was made. I didn't ask for it, but for some reason the barber had a publicity shot from the film's original release on his wall, and that's what he wanted me to look like. That was the way he knew me. It was also the way *I* knew me.

From the deep recess of a hall closet, I retrieved the original white parka with the green visor. It's one of the few items that I have kept for sentimental reasons since 1977. I plan to enter wearing it for my interview with Osborn. It should get a laugh, I'm thinking, but what if it doesn't? Maybe for those who are seeing the film for the first time it will spoil the surprise of it when it appears onscreen. I decide to bring it along with me to LA and ask the "powers that be" what they think. If it's good enough for The Apocalyptic Film Festival then it ought to be good enough for Turner Classic Movies.

A month later...

Instead of strolling in Central Park, I'm strolling on Hollywood Boulevard looking down, as everyone does, at the seemingly endless array of engraved names set in the pavement where people were stepping on them, practically twenty-four hours a day, seven days a week, every day of the year. There are names one has never heard of, names no one's thought of in decades, and brand new celebrities as well. The names are not always easy to read because they face in different directions, which causes folks to bump into each other a lot. Some poor soul is surely sleeping on somebody's name while wrapped in a blanket. I feel sorry for both of them.

The Walk of Fame, as it's known, is a big deal to millions of people all over the world who have a chance to feel connected to the past, as their memories are jabbed every four steps by another familiar person who lies at their feet, as if in a grave. The stars are dead, but they are remembered. They're in the past and the present at the same time and, oddly, they're being stepped on by millions of people they never even knew. Their names will be known for a long time, even if it's only by the nameless, faceless strangers parading above them in sneakers, sandals, and worn-out soles.

The five phases of an actor's career, referred to earlier in this tome meant something different to me when I first heard of them at the start of my career. The first one, "Who's Tony Roberts?" was immediately understood because, as far as show business was concerned, I was a complete non-entity. Fair enough. But the "Who's Tony Roberts?" that comes at the end is like trying to solve a Rubik's Cube. Any answer, or conclusions, that I might arrive at depend on where I'm standing. If I open my box of clippings (today it would be called a digital file in my storage cloud) I see myself as I was defined by critics, posters, photo ops, press releases, etc. On the other hand, if I revisit the work that can be seen on a screen, my reactions to it vary from embarrassment to a feeling that I got away with something. Most of what I did was on the stage and, except for a few instances when something was filmed, the work only exists as a memory in the minds of those who saw it.

Without getting too existential, "Who's Tony Roberts?" is the same question everybody asks themselves if they're lucky enough to have reached a certain age, when reflection seems the order of the day.

I still enjoy the work that comes my way. Much of that has been the recording of audiobooks, many of which are pulp fiction, but every now and then I get to do something classy, like Kurt Vonnegut's *Cat's Cradle*, or Kipling's *The Jungle Book*, or a book by Woodward & Bernstein. I even read an entire version of *Star Wars* after the film was released. The most fun to do was *The Maltese Falcon* which, like most film buffs, I've seen at least a dozen times. The book was almost the same as the screenplay, line for line, so every sentence had already been said with significance by Bogart, Lorre, and Greenstreet. Greenstreet was rough on the vocal chords, but there needed to be a hint of each of them in the final product, without it ever becoming a parody of anybody.

A piece of advice to aspiring audiobook readers: read five minutes of newsprint every day for two weeks into a tape recorder and listen to it back. You will learn more how to speak into a microphone than any class could ever teach.

I also recorded an unauthorized book about Frank Sinatra which was very coincidental. My father was the announcer for the Tommy Dorsey Band when Sinatra joined up with it in the early 1940s. He was also the announcer for Frank's CBS weekly television show in the 1950s. I remember being introduced to him at the doorway of his dressing room when I was twelve. His shirt was unbuttoned and he was thinner than anyone I had ever seen. I had never seen ribs before (except in a Chinese restaurant).

One night during the run of *Victor/ Victoria* it was rumored, and then confirmed, that Sinatra would be in the audience the upcoming Saturday night. Knowing this three days in advance gave me the chance to reinvigorate my six month old performance with the intent to plumb every nuance I could out of it. The next three shows, I couldn't imagine anything else while onstage, but that Frank Sinatra was sitting (in a good seat, no doubt) and watching my performance, laughing in all the right places, and admiring my vocal chops. Finally, it was Saturday night. I put all such thoughts aside and gave the truest and most un-self-conscious performance I could muster. I didn't expect Frank to come backstage, but it turned out that he had not felt well as he was entering the Marquis Theatre and was taken home without ever having heard the overture. Darn.

June, 2013

I'm sitting at the bar waiting for a friend at Sparks Steak House. On the shelf opposite me there's an array of bottles, but my eyes rest on one with the bold label

"Knob Creek." It's a fine old bourbon, which I don't happen to drink, but it reminds me that I do, however, portray a fictional protagonist who never drinks anything else. He's Stone Barrington, the hero in over twenty-five audiobooks that I've recorded over the past thirty years. I don't share a great many things in common with Stone. He flies airplanes, inherited a fortune (twice), is an ex-cop, and risks his life when asked to by his employers, a high end New York City law firm and a security contractor named Strategic Services. People get shot, stabbed, blown up, and poisoned. Stone also meets up with a lot of women.

I, on the other hand, prefer martinis straight up to bourbon on the rocks and, as I've said, I'm not too crazy about heights, so I don't fly a plane. Of course, in my profession I also meet up with a lot of women, but unlike Stone's, most of them aren't spies or murderers. As far as I know.

Stone is the longest running character I have ever played, and the one the least number of people know about, but every so often someone at a checkout counter or hotel desk will say, "You have such a familiar voice. Do you do commercials, or audiobooks?"

"I do the Stuart Woods books. I'm Stone Barrington." If that rings a bell, I'm then asked to speak a few words as Dino Bacchetti, Stone's sidekick. Dino is still a cop and has a familiarly raspy, back-throated, pinched delivery that'll cut through anything. He brings a blue-collar sarcasm to the goings-on, along with a thick Brooklyn accent. I've often regretted that I so casually chose that Dino sounds the way he does. It's pretty harsh on the vocal chords, and I never expected him to reappear so often. He and Stone have a real bromance going on. Stone is a piece of cake to do because, as the wonderful actress Marian Seldes once advised me, "Always use your own voice and intonations for the leading character, whether it's Sam Spade, or Abraham Lincoln. It grounds things."

Since I am the voice of all the other characters in the book, I want each of them to sound unique. There are many ethnicities and nationalities represented, and several women's voices for which I try to pitch my own slightly higher and thinner. Certain events are deliberately steamy and good fodder for the overacting often inspired by pulp-fiction material. Despite the laughs provoked by the dialogue among those of us in the studio, at least one clean take has to make the grade before we can move on to the next chapter. It has to have conviction and credibility. It's not always easy, but at least the finished product exists in some permanent way. It's an audiobook. It can live on a shelf somewhere.

Stage acting is like sculpting in ice. As soon as it's accomplished, it melts away. It's ephemeral, not like a book, or a painting, or anything else that's tangible. Acting exists in the moment—it has its effect and leaves an impression that may reverberate for decades or vanish into thin air. It depends on the belief invested in it, as well as the sensibilities of those who witness it. It doesn't help that an audience today is seen (by producers in all media) through the eyes of a demographic profile. Families used to gather before the TV set and watch *The Ed Sullivan Show* because that's all that was on, and it included something for everyone. There was a little opera, some stand-up, a pop star, a magician, etc. Now each family member has their own television set or device, and watches a program designed to appeal to their particular interests. The concern I have with this is that one's interests don't expand the way they used to, and we cease to share a common response to almost anything. Add this to the availability of the internet and it's clear why it is so difficult to muster a large audience that will pay attention to anything other than the latest internationally broadcast natural disaster, or a Presidential address. We are a diverse mass of splintered sensibilities. It used to be that the theatre brought us together, but the new technologies seem to be scattering us into isolated consumer groups without much in common except to share a culture governed by the lowest common denominator. It's my theory that computer technology is already altering the way we participate in the world as drastically as the invention of the automobile did. We did gain a way to expand our physical environment, but perhaps at the cost of how we once perceived our relationship to our homes, or villages, or even to each other. Now we can all be in touch with each other all the time, which may cost us real intimacy, the kind of intimacy that people share in a theatre.

May, 2014

My agent sends me a screenplay about a case of child molestation that takes place in an Orthodox Yeshiva located across the bridge in Williamsburg, Brooklyn, the home of the Hasidic community. The picture is what is known as a "Low Budget Indie" which means there's no money, and it could turn out to be dreadful. It also means that it's unlikely to ever be released or distributed by a major producer or studio. This little film will take four weeks to shoot without any of the frills and trimmings that can make location shooting comfortable. It will adopt the tactics of "gorilla filming" capturing the authentic backgrounds where the story takes place.

This project could also turn out to be a gem, a gift from the Gods! I'll have to audition for it on camera for the writer and the director at a casting office on the Upper West Side. I would play a Rabbi confronted with a difficult moral dilemma. Although he has committed no crime himself, he is hard pressed by many in his congregation to cover up another's crime, rather than report it to the proper civic authority. It was just the sort of role I had been hoping for; deep and meaningful, yet relevant to Yeshivas, Churches, universities, and even the military.

I studied the script and memorized the sides that accompanied the full screenplay. I decided that a plain white shirt with a black blazer was the best I could do to look like a Rabbi at close range, but there was no time to grow a beard. I opened a drawer in my apartment and removed a yarmulke I had brought home from Marvin Hamlisch's recent memorial service. I put it in my pocket and hopped a cab to the West Side. Halfway across the park transverse it dawned on me that now was the perfect moment to step into character. I put on the yarmulke and began to imagine myself in the Rabbi's circumstances. Ten minutes later, I was a few feet from the lens and someone said, "Action." I was stunned to hear myself speaking in an unfamiliar voice. It was me, but it was me speaking in a hushed and sorrowful tone and with a Yiddish accent. Where did *that* come from? It may have come from my maternal grandmother's father who was a Rabbi himself, but never made it out of Russia.

Fade in, fade out, I got the part! Even better, the film wasn't scheduled to begin shooting until mid-August so I had more than three months to prepare, and I did. I became a student of Orthodox Judaism. I read books I never thought I would about the earliest emergence of Jewish identity. I learned about the papyrus scrolls that were found by the Nile River, written in Hebrew, documenting the events that shaped history. I even visited a Rabbi in Williamsburg and was welcomed into the homes of some local residents. Their customs, and habits, were as foreign to me as if they lived on the other side of the world, which isn't so strange because that's where their traditions began.

After three months of ardent preparation I had memorized the entire part from start to finish. There were scenes of quiet emotional intensity and scenes involving long orations before large groups of students. I had bored my close friends with my newfound knowledge of all things Judaic and was ready for someone to yell, "Action!"

I forgot to mention that the creative team for this film had advised me not to bother letting my hair grow or to sprout a beard because their hair and make-up team would design a "look" for me that would authenticate the Hasidic traditions. I had achieved a few new benchmarks; I had memorized more dialogue than I had ever done before for a film, I was finally going to have to speak some Hebrew, and I was going to be rendered completely unrecognizable! What a wonderful challenge. It felt like I was being reinvented.

However, and this is a big however, a week before shooting was to begin, I was informed that the whole project was off. Cancelled. *Maybe* just delayed. Perhaps it would get its act together in seven or eight months. Sure. That's showbiz.

I'm not sorry for the chance to have learned so much about the many issues that this project touched on. It was a gift, even if it never gets done. There have been many other projects that *got* done that should not have. They were not gifts. They were just product.

December, 2014

Hallelujah! Suddenly my phone is ringing. It's the way it has always been in my career. It's just that the ups and downs are more spread out now, but the contrast in the work coming my way is hard to figure. This time I'm offered a first-class round-trip to LA for two days of work on a comedy special for the Cartoon Network to be shot in live action. That means it's not a cartoon. It's a program aimed at adults that will air late at night. The fee is enough to make it worthwhile and it's a chance to catch up with some friends and relatives on the West Coast. I'm also told the material is a little blue, but nothing I should worry about. This is a far cry from the high-minded script that came my way a few months ago, about the Rabbi, which was never "green-lit," as the insiders like to say.

Accepting this new offer reminds me of the old joke about the man who offers an attractive woman one hundred dollars if she'll sleep with him and she says:

"A hundred dollars? What do you think I am? Now, if you offered me five thousand, that would be different!"

"Well, now that we've established what you are, it's just a matter of setting the price."

I know very few actors who haven't felt like a whore from time to time. I certainly did when I clawed in the duck mud for Disney and hung from the ceiling in Jamaica, but it's even more humbling to be directed by the ad execs in the control room during the recording of a voice-over commercial. Every actor I know hates that the most. They want you to say the lines *their* way, instead of what your own instincts are telling you. I used to plead with them to let me assume as natural a tone as I could, as if I were speaking to just one person through the microphone, but the salesmen have their own ideas about which words to stress, or bury, and usually end up with something sounding artificial. The sessions produce a compromised final product that satisfies the different opinions held by the people in the room, i.e. the client, the producer, the writer, etc. The actor is the one who must deliver a reading that "makes everybody happy." It is not uncommon to do thirty takes for a one-line commercial. Nevertheless, more money flows into actors' pockets from voice-over work than from any other employment source.

An early bit of advice I got from my father (where else?) about making commercials: "When you're in that recording booth, you must think of yourself as a whore, because that's how they expect you to behave. They're paying you to do what they want. Know that going in, and don't give anybody a hard time. Do whatever you can to please them. That's what a whore is supposed to do. When it's over you'll have the last laugh because you'll smile all the way to the bank."

But, I digress. I'm delighted to hear the word "offer" rather than "audition" and look forward to being in LA. It's been a few years. I wonder if I can still get a reservation at my favorite steak joint on Santa Monica Boulevard? Will the old staff still be there? I was once a regular customer. I would hate to show up and be ushered away, as I've seen happen to so many others. If I phone ahead my name might not ring a bell with the guy who takes reservations. He's probably twenty-five years old anyway and doesn't have a clue as to who I am. I make an elaborate plan to ask a woman I know with an authoritarian voice to call on my behalf and list a few of my credits, to make sure I get a table.

All in all, I'm happy because there's action! The low budget indy, the Stone Barrington novels, and the gig in LA are evidence of the fact that I am still in the game, so to speak, still alive, and still a working actor, which it was always my ambition to become.

Fate has somehow offered me a chance to play myself in a groundbreaking, new comedic format which I completely failed to understand the first time I read it. According to the script, I am introduced as myself—Tony Roberts. I am supposed to be the authentic me, portraying the father of the leading character who has written his own life into a hilarious but also troubling fantasy. It requires that I come up with a good performance as myself in the early scenes.

As I ponder which version of myself to present under these circumstances, it occurs to me that I should probably go into the same mode as when greeting fans after the show. Gracious, humble, but keeping something back for myself. I know that will get me through it, but I wonder if by doing so I might be cheating myself of the opportunity to fly a little higher. What if I permit myself to experience an honest sense of discomfort by trying to be "Tony Roberts?" I let that idea sink in for a while and realize there's no limit to where my imagination may roam in exploring what's deeply funny about the predicament I'm in. It's an existential conversation: Who am I, and what am I doing here? At all costs my behavior has to ring true and be honest. I like the challenge of it. It resonates Pirandello. They're also paying me. I have no complaints.

A woman of about seventy walks towards me as I'm crossing the street near where I've lived for the last thirty-five years. She smiles, knowingly. I am aware that she recognizes me, and I am ready to go into my customary gracious reception of her compliment, whatever it might be.

"Well," she says with a hint of surprise in her voice, "I haven't seen *you* in a long time!" And she keeps going.

Unless I can simulate the 360 degree head spin so artfully performed in *The Exorcist* there is no way I can offer any response to her. I wanted to say, with a slight edge to it, "Well where have you *been*?" I wanted to tell her that I had just returned from Los Angeles where I had the opportunity to act in a brand new groundbreaking comedy that was stretching the boundaries of the television medium by mingling the elements of farce and terror in previously unimagined ways. By that time she was already a half a block away and it would have been rude of me. I wanted her to know that her remark, although unintended, had wounded me. Or maybe I was just being paranoid. Fortunately, the street light changed and I never had the chance to confront her with any of this nonsense.

My mother would pose the question at times, "What if you meet a friend on the street and he says, 'Gee, Tony, I haven't seen you in ages. You look terrific. Things must be going really well for you. Keep it up!' But a few minutes later you might meet another friend and this one says, 'Gosh, Tony, what's happened to you? You look as if you've been to hell and back. You look as if you could use a new lease on life!'" My mother would ask, "Did you change? Aren't you the same person regardless of how differently you may be perceived?" Thus, making the point that it's unreliable to put too much trust in whatever anyone perceives you to be. The only assessment that matters is your own, but when all is said and done, who among us is able to rely solely on one's own evaluation for comfort and reassurance? No one has ever been *that* lucky.

Lee Strasberg told me when I was sixteen to go to college and get my "stage legs." I think he meant that I should learn how to feel comfortable in my own skin in front of a live audience. At one time I was going to call this memoir *Stage Legs*, but I had another meaning in mind. Whereas "sea legs" refers to the ability to keep one's balance on the deck of a ship being tossed at sea, "stage legs" has come to mean to me, the ability to keep one's balance in order to survive the ups and downs of show business.

All careers in show business are a balancing act between the need for self-expression and the need to earn a living. A long career is full of celebrations and humiliations, but that's hardly too much to endure for being a working actor. I could not foresee when I began my journey that I would be employed for years in musical comedies because I could adequately sing and dance, and I did not know that my work in meaningful theatre would be largely subsidized by income derived from voice-over commercials.

Why does anyone want to act anyway? Voltaire said, "Illusion is the first of all pleasures." Is it a prerequisite if you want to become an actor? Do people in other walks of life (meaning "civilians") carry within them the same level of self consciousness as we do, or must an actor have an abundance of self-involvement in order to convincingly put flesh and bones on an array of fictional characters? Does this facility come with a cost? An actor's ability to slip in and out of character might have unforeseen side effects. We may dramatize our own lives as well as the lives of the characters we're cast to play. Ultimately, as Shakespeare and Beckett both point out, we are all actors in some play we can only guess the meaning of.

Although I've never had the opportunity to give an acceptance speech, the most eloquent one I can remember was one given by Bette Davis upon receiving something akin to a lifetime achievement award. She said, "I am thrilled to receive this honor, but feel it is undeserved. I am someone who's dream came true. I wanted to be an actress and I became one." I may be paraphrasing a bit, but basically that was her message. In the same vein I often think of what a great idol of mine, Orson Welles declared at various times during his career; that it was the work that really mattered to him. Everything else that had to do with visibility, stardom, success, reviews, etc, was ancillary. In the end it was the challenge of the task at hand, or work itself that was the greatest reward. In spite of that outlook he still had to admit that the good reviews he received were always a relief, but only brought a passing sense of accomplishment. The bad reviews tended to linger longer until the pain they inflicted wore off. But I am one who had the great opportunity to enjoy the work of acting and nothing could ever beat that.

I inherited a lot because of the circumstances I found myself in throughout my entire life. There were certainly setbacks, but I also had tremendous advantages. Chief among them and not really mentioned in this account is the matter of my father's voice. This was something different from becoming conditioned by his secular liberal persuasions, and practical concerns. This came with the DNA. As I watched a promo on TCM recently for "Swing Time," a 1930s film starring Fred Astaire and Ginger Rogers, I was startled to hear my father's voice doing the narration. It was his alright, and it was heard several times during the next week. I don't know when it was recorded and it had no financial value to anybody at this juncture, but there he was as mellow, buoyant, and enthusiastic as ever. He never tutored me about how to place my voice, or how to command attention when I spoke, but it must have had a primal affect on me because it instilled a sense of authority into my vocal delivery which has stood me in good stead. He deserves the credit for this, or nature itself for which I can only be eternally grateful. I inherited my father's voice, and perhaps even fulfilled his unrealized dream: to become an actor…and survive.

The "powers that be" suggest that my memoir is a little short in length by most standards. This is probably due to the fact that I have kept the focus on my journey as an actor, rather than venturing into areas of my life that I prefer to keep private. I've deliberately stayed away from my "love life," and have not indulged in any kind of "score settling" or in telling stories meant to embarrass or humiliate anybody.

When I told Max that I was writing it he paused for a moment and said, "Who's gonna read it?" It was the towel snapping thing again.

"My many fans!" I reply, calling him a dirty name at the same time. "The people who stop me in the street, who may have seen me in some show, or who are curious to learn something about what it means to be an actor and still make a living."

In actuality, I think I wrote this memoir for other actors. I don't believe my love affair with acting is any different from that of my peers. This is the conclusion I've arrived at after several decades in the business. When actors are hired they make a pledge to one another; they promise to make believe as if it's really "cops and robbers" all over again. The bargain they arrive at, in most circumstances, is this: you believe as fully as your skills will allow, in the story we're supposed to be telling, and I'll believe in it just as much. Somewhere in the middle our imaginations will find the aesthetic truth of the moment, scene, story, etc., and we'll be on solid ground. The solid ground is the thing that lets the audience put aside their own reality for the duration of our play, and become informed, and maybe even enlightened by witnessing it.

When this connection between actors takes place it is the equivalent of the home run that gets hit in all soporific adolescent fantasies. The actors are locked into "let's pretend" (ironically, the most popular show on the radio when I was ten years-old was called *Let's Pretend.* It was also the program my father announced every Saturday morning and where I first saw grown-ups "act out").

March, 2015

When I was still a pre-teen I would stand on the beach at Fire Island where the water met the sand and sing "Soliloquy" into the wind. I don't know why the passionate soliloquy from *Carousel* had such an impact on me, but it did. It was my favorite song long before I even started dating. Ten years later, at Northwestern University, I would be cast in a production of *Liliom* by Ferenc Molnar, the play on which *Carousel* is based. I was to play Linzman, named Boscom in the musical, who is the victim of a robbery carried out by the hero Billy Bigalow. To the surprise of all Linzman is toting a gun to protect the payroll he is taking to his factory and foils the hold-up. Billy, not wanting to be arrested uses his own weapon, a knife, to commit suicide. Mine was a small role, but my first at Northwestern and it made a favorable impression. Now, fifty-five years later, I have been cast to play the Starkeeper who Billy meets after he has died, but before he is admitted to heaven. In *Liliom* the character is referred to as a police magistrate, although he can just as easily be thought of as Saint Peter. Whatever he's called, he is the embodiment of a benevolent spirit, who persuades Billy to journey back to earth and do something "real fine" to redeem his shameful abdication of responsibility regarding his daughter's life on earth.

It's certainly a challenge to play a supernatural character, or entity who has the powers to qualify, or disqualify anybody from entering heaven depending on their earthly experience. It means finding a conviction strong enough to support the belief in a benevolent, or at least a fair, and just universe. That's a lot to ask, but it's the basis of all religion: the idea that hope is not unfounded. This is what makes *Carousel* a tragedy, in the classic sense. Something is lost forever, but there is still a transcendent wisdom that delivers a catharsis for the audience.

This leads me to write about a mysterious phenomena that many of my fellow actors have made note of, as have I. It is the sudden trip that begins the moment a job has been secured. Even before the ink is dry on a contract I begin to unconsciously become the character I've been cast to portray. Before I have even pored over the script to define the theme of the piece my subconscious is already selecting qualities in my own personality which align with those of my new fictional avatar. This "becoming" is the beginning of what will eventually show up on the stage, or screen. It happens automatically. One's imagination is already on the bike, or the horse, on the way to mesh oneself to the character the playwright has sketched out in the script. The deeper the affinity, the more convincing and seamless the performance will be.

What better toy could one be given than to be asked to play God toward the end of one's life? Gradually, the enormity of the task seeps its way into my process. I must delve into the deepest sources of my positive belief to counter the otherwise negative implications of an immoral universe. The Starkeeper is really saying: "Have hope!" It's the opposite of Beckett. I can't help but believe that being given this role at this point in my life is a blessing. True, it's a small role, (Alvina Krause used to say: "There are no small roles, there are only small actors!") and there's no singing or dancing required, but it has the soul of the world in it. If I can bring it off, it's a chance to "hit one over the fence!" One could almost believe there is some kind of providence at work here.

How strange to be surfing channels as I'm having my morning cereal and glance up at the television to see a familiar face. At first I'm not sure who it belongs to, but then it dawns on me that it's *me!* I'm about thirty years-old and the love interest of a character known as "Julie" in an episode of *The Love Boat* (my agent at the time didn't think it was such a good idea to accept the part. "You don't want to be on *The Love Boat*," he chided. "*Love Boat* is for dead people").

The show was a big hit at the time, and over the years audiences who live south of the Mason-Dixon line knew me more from that show than from any other venue. I know this because on many visits to Disneyland with my daughter I was frequently recognized as Julie's boyfriend. Most of them had never even seen a Woody Allen movie.

It's unusual to be reminded so suddenly of a moment so far in the past. Turner Classic Movies is an album of past performances which now exist in the present. Here it is at breakfast staring me in the face. It's nice to be reminded of the past, but also slightly unsettling because it's a reminder of all the other things that have happened that one doesn't remember. So be it.

All I know is I was never happier than on a day one summer far away from the Great White Way or Hollywood when I was driving along a country road in my all-time favorite little Rabbit Convertible. I'd closed the night before in Anton Chekov's *The Seagull* in Saratoga, and would start rehearsing the next day in *Guys & Dolls* in Pittsburgh. It was late July and the top was down. The luggage compartment was too small for baggage, so my duffle bag and make-up case filled the rear seat. I remember singing that song from *Pinocchio*, the one that goes, "Hi-diddle-dee-dee, an actor's life for me!" Everything seemed right with the world.

As I drove through this rural setting, where cornfields stretched out endlessly on both sides of the road, it occurred to me that I had no purpose whatsoever in this environment so removed from my usual haunts, but I did sense a connection to generations of traveling players who ventured forth to bring diversion or enlightenment and, unfortunately, sometimes even tedium, to hopefully expectant audiences.

A hundred years ago I might have borne the stigma of a vagabond, but now, I had a duly signed and executed Actors' Equity contract in the glove compartment and was on my way to a new gig. For any actor, this is a rare and privileged circumstance. "Hi-diddle-dee-dee," indeed!

Acknowledgements

Thanks to all my friends who took the time to read bits and pieces of this opus and made helpful suggestions. You know who you are. Apologies to those not named who I have learned from, laughed with, and shared the wings with.

Special thanks to Steven Ferezy, my copy editor.

CPSIA information can be obtained at www.ICGtesting.com
Printed in the USA
BVOW06*0429100915

417315BV00002B/14/P